ANSWERING A

FUNDAMENTALIST

FUNDAMENTALIST

ALBERT J. NEVINS, M.M.

Our Sunday Visitor Publishing Division
Our Sunday Visitor, Inc.
Huntington, Indiana 46750

International Standard Book Number: 0-87973-433-7
Library of Congress Catalog Card Number: 90-60644

Cover design by the Aslan Group, Ltd., Atlanta, Ga.

Published in the United States of America

433

Contents

Preface

This book is written for modern fundamentalists, not for Protestant evangelicals who are already in dialogue with the Catholic Church and who spring from Pietist and Wesleyan traditions. Although fundamentalists and evangelicals have a great deal in common, particularly their view of the Bible, evangelicalism has developed a theology which today's fundamentalist lacks.

In a sense this book is badly titled, since fundamentalists are not looking for answers, believing that they already have *The Answer* — the Bible. What this work hopes to show is that there are some answers beyond the Bible; after all, the Church was in existence for many years before the New Testament was completed. This book will make frequent reference to the Bible, drawing on its wisdom and truth, not in an attempt to match quotations with the fundamentalist, but to show that the Bible is far broader than some selected texts which have been handed down from a long anti-Catholic conditioning.

This book does not question fundamentalist sincerity or the fundamentalists' love of Jesus. Their relationship with the Lord is one that Christians outside their belief would do well to imitate.

Fundamentalists have brought many people to Christ and have given those people's lives purpose. Hence it is a sadness that these people of the Lord condemn so harshly what they only imagine they know. Their mental picture of the Catholic Church is beyond reality.

This book is a plea for the fundamentalist to consider with an open mind; it seeks only truth, the Catholic Church's reasoning about itself, in the hope that the arguments will be found both logical and scriptural. The Catholic Church is rapidly nearing one billion adherents, and it only makes sense to try to understand what this vast number believe and why they believe what they believe.

It is also an entreaty to former Catholics who have left the Church for fundamentalism to consider what they have departed. It is not the purpose of this book to delve into psychological or sociological reasons why they have left the faith of their fathers, but for this author, who has spoken to some former Catholics, it was evident that they never truly had faith in their Church or were never really educated in the Faith in which they were born, sometimes despite a Catholic-school education.

This book is also meant for Catholics in the hope that they will better understand that the cause of their beliefs is the Lord Himself, and that it will lead to greater appreciation of what they have been given through the great mercy of the Holy Spirit. We can always use a review of our beliefs.

What we have tried to do in this book is to take major fundamentalist objections, as found in their literature, and use them as jumping-off places. As this book demonstrates, it takes only a brief sentence or two to make a charge that requires a reply of pages for even a brief answer. Indeed, some of the objections are subjects of whole books, and more detailed explanations will be found in the bibliography in the back of this volume.

Fruitful reading! May the Holy Spirit guide your thoughts!

A.J.N.

1

The Fundamentalist Phenomenon

It is not easy to define fundamentalism today, because this new phenomenon of an older methodology takes varied shapes and forms. Traditional fundamentalism still exists among Baptists and Presbyterians outside urban areas. Evangelicals are from the fundamentalist tradition but part from what might properly be called neofundamentalism, the form that exists today.

Fundamentalism as a religious movement had its start in Victorian England as a reaction to the new religious liberalism that developed from the secularist teachings of Charles Darwin and Sigmund Freud — one taking God out of nature, the other removing God from the human psyche. Conservative believers of various denominations were horrified at the inroads of these materialistic beliefs in school and church, and in contradistinction to long-held religious principles. They interpreted the propagation of these new ideas as an attack that threatened the very foundations of the Bible and as a denial of Christian doctrine. They saw ministers of their own creeds and Christian theologians being swept up in the scientific thought that had come into style, and they accused them of recasting Christian teaching.

In 1909 a group of proponents of orthodox faith organized, both in protest and defense, to make their position known through the issuing of *The Fundamentals*. These publications, which lasted about two years, gave five points of doctrine upon which orthodox Christians, now called Fundamentalists, could never yield:

1. The virgin birth,
2. Physical resurrection of Jesus,
3. Inerrancy of Scripture,
4. Christ's sacrificial atonement for sin,
5. The Second Coming of Christ

Both in Europe and America, the movement brought together people from various Churches who sought to have the Fundamentals included in their own creeds. They opposed ministers who did not agree with them, set up their own organs of promotion, and in America even brought their beliefs into politics, demanding in effect a Christian loyalty oath, wrapped in Americanism and the Bible. Fundamentalists in New York City created a cause célèbre in their attacks on Dr. Harry Emerson Fosdick, a preacher of great reputation and following. Dr. Fosdick, despite being a Baptist, had been appointed the governing minister of New York City's First Presbyterian Church. His modernist preaching brought down the wrath of the fundamentalists, and in a well-publicized show of strength they forced Fosdick's resignation from his prominent pulpit.

But the pulpit was not the only point of attack. School curricula came under the fundamentalist microscope. They selected an obscure Tennessee school teacher, J. T. Scopes, and accused him of teaching the theory of evolution. In what became known worldwide as the Monkey Trial, they sued to have Scopes dismissed. The fundamentalists chose as their lawyer a very distinguished American, William Jennings Bryan, a skilled orator but at the time an old man. The school district chose as its counsel the celebrated lawyer Clarence Darrow, who had won his reputation defending unpopular causes. Bryan won the case, but in doing so he was mocked, jeered at, and humiliated by Darrow. The old warrior died five days later in his sleep, his death brought about, fundamentalists averred, by the treatment he had received from the evolutionists.

Fundamentalism as a national crusade began to peter out along with the arrival of the Great Depression which started under President Hoover. It lost considerable strength in the North, Midwest, and West, although it remained a force in the South. World War II put it on a hiatus. The movement gained new momentum in the 1960s, partly as a response to the anti-Americanism brought about by the Vietnam War, partly because of the growing power of television which was seen as amoral, partly because of the secularism that was affecting society, particularly the public school system, and (some think) as a response to the civil rights movement. At any rate, the times were disturbed, and fundamentalism was ready with simple answers.

The original fundamentalism in the United States had drawn its strength from the mainline Churches. Its resurrection has come in splinter groups with such names as Living Word, Bible Chapel, Faith Tabernacle, Calvary Chapel, Covenant Missionary Church, New Church of God, Blessed Hope Christian Church, Gospel Assembly, Full Gospel Church, Christ's Tabernacle, and so on. These groups are independent of one another, usually formed by a charismatic leader with an outreach program. They meet in small wooden or cinderblock churches for emotionally charged services with lots of hugging and fervent singing, testimonies by the saved, and a moving sermon by the evangelist, usually about sin and the salvation offered by Jesus. Most services conclude with a fiery exhortation for the unsaved to come forward and commit themselves to Jesus and His salvation, which is assured them on acceptance of the invitation.

Because of the large number of these splinter churches, it is difficult to define this new fundamentalism. While they accept the five Fundamentals, most seem to place primary emphasis on Bible inerrancy and a sixth fundamental, anti-Catholicism. However, direction is given by the leader who often has his own "hot buttons," who is usually self-appointed as founder and organizer, and who may or may not have had formal scriptural and theological training. These churches look to olden times when the world was not so complex and seek simple answers in black and white. This leads to a simplistic approach to the world, which is seen as evil, and the kingdom of God as the only good.

This resurrection of Manichaeanism sometimes leads to dire results. A recent publicized court trial was brought against a fundamentalist church and its leader by the parents of a young man who had committed suicide because he could no longer live surrounded by evil, yet who committed an evil greater than his imagined evils by usurping God's dominion over human life. The parents won the case, but a court of law is not the place for a decision in an important theological question. It is not the world that is evil but many people in it who need conversion to Jesus Christ. God created the world "and saw how good it was" (Gn 1:25), and He gave man stewardship over His creation, not to condemn it as evil but to see and cherish its goodness.

One of the more serious problems that can be found in many of these splinter sects is that they lead to self-deception. Each group believes it alone has apostolic truth, that all others have departed from this truth. They fail to say where Jesus or the Holy Spirit was all those centuries until their group was formed — Jesus who had promised His Church, "I am with you always, to the close of the age" (Mt 28:20). And the Holy Spirit, whom Jesus promised would be in His Church to keep it from all error (Jn 15:16, etc.). "Always" means continually and constantly. It does not mean being present in the Apostolic Church and then disappearing for almost two thousand years until His presence came alive again in someone's idea of what His Church should be.

Perhaps the greatest self-deception is in the matter of faith which fundamentalists believe they give to God by their born again testimony. But we do not give faith to God. God gives faith to us through His revelation, and when He makes this gift, through no merits of our own, He grants us the necessary grace to accept and live this faith, as long as we cooperate with His grace in doing His will. "Not everyone who says to me, 'Lord, Lord' shall enter the kingdom of heaven, but he who does the will of my Father who is in heaven. On that day many will say to me, 'Lord, Lord, did we not prophesy in your name, and do many mighty works in your name?' And then will I declare to them, 'I never knew you; depart from me, you evildoers' " (Mt 7:21-23). This is a text that demands considerable understanding.

Because of inroads fundamentalists were making in their states, the Catholic bishops of Alabama and Mississippi issued a joint pastoral letter to their people, pointing out the dangers. They warned Catholics to be aware of the blandishments the doctrine offered because of its simplistic approach to spiritual problems. They listed these temptations as:

1. An unreasonable certainty about the meaning of Scripture texts regardless of their content.

2. An overly simplistic certainty of salvation, achieved instantly upon acceptance of Christ as savior.

3. A deep sense of personal security, often in identifying the "American way" with God's call and will.

4. Intimacy with God in a relationship so personal that it excludes others.

Fundamentalists have made the Bible into a sort of reference encyclopedia that answers all questions of life, when in fact it is the story of God's revealing and saving presence among us. The Bible makes known God's plan of salvation for us, culminating in the revelation of His Son, Jesus Christ, who left behind Him, when He returned to the Father, the ordinary means He willed for the salvation of the people entrusted to Him by the Father. The task of the Christian is to know and live that plan. The spiritual blindness caused by anti-Catholicism is hiding it from multitudes.

It is not the purpose of this book to make an overall and detailed critique of fundamentalism but to respond to the most common objections fundamentalists make against the Catholic Church. That we will now proceed to do.

2

The Bible

The Bible is the inspired and literal word of God and the sole rule of faith. Catholics are not people of the book because the institutional church keeps it from them. The entirety of the Bible is true, trustworthy, and dependable even in matters not related to doctrine or salvation. In pre-Reformation days Catholics chained the Bible and resisted attempts to translate and distribute it. In modern times the Roman church in a concession to common views has made the Bible available but done little to encourage its reading. Consequently, lay Catholics — and sorry to say, most priests — remain totally ignorant of the Word of God.

Catholics and the Bible

The position of the Catholic Church on sacred Scripture was summarized by the bishops of the Church at Vatican Council II, which enlarged on the teaching of the Council of Trent and Vatican Council I. The Council Fathers said in their *Constitution on Divine Revelation* (n. 11):

"The divinely revealed realities, which are contained and presented in the text of sacred Scripture, have been written down under the inspiration of the Holy Spirit. For Holy Mother Church, relying on the faith of the apostolic age, accepts as sacred and canonical the books of the Old and New Testaments, whole and entire, with all their parts, on the grounds that, written under the inspiration of the Holy Spirit (cf. Jn 20:31; 2 Tim

3:16; 2 Pet 1:19-21, 3:15-16), they have God as their author and have been handed on as such to the Church herself."

Further on, the same document says: "Since they [the sacred books] are inspired by God and committed to writing once and for all time, they present God's own Word in an unalterable form, and they make the voice of the Holy Spirit sound again and again in the words of the prophets and apostles. It follows that all the preaching of the Church, as indeed the entire Christian religion, should be nourished and ruled by sacred Scripture. In the sacred books the Father who is in heaven comes lovingly to meet his children, and talks with them. . . . Access to sacred Scripture ought to be open wide to the Christian faithful" (n. 21).

This official statement by all the bishops of the Church refutes the charge that the Catholic Church "second-rates" the Bible and discourages its members from reading it. Indeed, it was the Catholic Church which preserved the Bible as we know it from apostolic times until the sixteenth century, when the Protestant Reformation began to make changes in it.

The saying that the Church does nothing to encourage Bible reading is only made from ignorance. Most Catholic parishes today offer classes in Bible studies. To encourage the reading of Sacred Scripture, the Church grants a partial indulgence to Catholics who, with veneration due the divine word, make a spiritual reading from the Bible. A plenary indulgence is granted each day if this reading is continued for at least half an hour. To take advantage of modern biblical research, the American bishops authorized a new translation of the Bible, now known as the New American Bible. This is approved for liturgical use, as is the Jerusalem Bible. A number of other translations, made in common by Catholic and Protestant scholars, such as the Revised Standard Version, are also approved for Catholic use.

The central act of Catholic worship is the Mass, which is composed of two main parts: the Liturgy of the Word and the

Liturgy of the Eucharist. Attendance at both parts is necessary for a Catholic to fulfill the Sunday obligation. The Liturgy of the Word consists of three Scripture readings, one from the Old Testament, one from the Epistles, and a third from the Gospels, plus one of the Psalms. These readings are assigned for Sundays in a three-year cycle and weekdays in a two-year cycle, designed in this time to cover the entire Bible. These readings are proclaimed at Mass by a lay lector, deacon, or priest, with the Gospel always reserved for the latter two. In addition, the readings are followed by a homily delivered by deacon or priest, which is an explanation of the Scriptures which have just been read and their practicalization to daily life. Jimmy Swaggart's charge that Catholic priests "are not trained in the Word of God" and "know little more about it than the layman" is ridiculous in its absurdity. Catholic seminary training consists of four years of college and another four years of post-graduate studies, and Sacred Scripture is a major course. Some priests are sent on for advanced degrees in Scripture. The Catholic Church's leading biblical scholars become members of the Pontifical Biblical Institute in Rome, which has the mission of promoting biblical studies and keeping translations from error.

The History of the Bible

Few Protestants stop to realize that it was the Catholic Church which defined the Bible, selected the books found in the New Testament canon, and kept this word of God free from error. This is a remarkable achievement when it is considered that the entire Bible had to be copied by hand — a very time-consuming and painstaking job. Yet when modern translations are compared with the Dead Sea scrolls, which go back to the time of Christ, we can realize how accurately these copies were made. Bibles were copied by hand by monks in monasteries. These copies were kept in monasteries, abbeys, cathedrals, and universities for use by priests and scholars. Because of the expense of such volumes, it was a very rare layman who possessed an entire Bible. The charge has been made that Catholics chained the Bible. In some places they did — not to prevent people from reading it but to prevent unauthorized persons from carrying it off. Also it must be remembered that only the educated could read or write and these were a minority. The majority of the people had to depend upon preaching to become familiar with the Bible. This changed about 1440, when Gutenberg invented moveable type and Bibles could be printed in greater quantity.

The Old Testament

The composition of the Old Testament as we know it today is a complex story, and the formation of its canon (list of inspired books) took many centuries. In the thirteenth to eleventh centuries B.C. the Jews gathered their traditions, particularly as they applied to Moses. During this period Jewish law and early poetry were also gathered. In the tenth century B.C. these traditions were put into writing, the stories about David were assembled, and the Psalms began to be used in Temple worship. However, it was not until the fifth century (c. 400 B.C.) that the Pentateuch (or Torah) was completed and recognized. The Pentateuch included the first five books of the Old Testament. Over these years other writings were also gathered — in the twelfth century the traditions that would make up Judges and Samuel down to the second century when Esther and Daniel were composed. However, the Jewish canon of the Old Testament was not settled until the Christian era had begun.

As early as 200 B.C. the Jewish Bible began to be translated into Greek. This became the work of rabbis and scholars in Alexandria and was known as the Septuagint (Greek for "seventy"), a name given because of what is now regarded as a spurious letter which said it was the work of seventy-two scholars, done in seventy-two days. This collection is also known as the Alexandrian Canon. This version was used by Hellenistic Jews and was the version used by St. Paul and others in the Apostolic Church. It is important to critics today because it is the translation of texts which have long been lost in the original.

It was the text the Catholic Church used in assembling the Christian Bible. It is still used by the Eastern Church. (St. Jerome in his translation of the Vulgate returned to Hebrew and Aramaic texts preserved among the Jews). The Catholic Bible when it was finally completed accepted forty-six books as making up the Old Testament. This list was approved by a number of early Church councils and declared a matter of faith at the Council of Trent.

Another canon came into being among the Jews, some suggesting that it was drawn up in response to the Christian canon, while others believe it resulted because of a dispute between Pharisees and other Jewish sects. After the destruction of Jerusalem by the Romans, a Jewish religious school was set up at Jamnia, a town west of Jerusalem. Here a group of rabbis worked on a canon of Jewish scripture, known as the Palestinian Canon, which numbered twenty-four sacred books, although Jews continued to read non-included books which were regarded as sacred. These books were called deuterocanonical (another canon). It was the Palestinian Canon which became the basis of the Protestant Bible, which consisted of thirty-nine books.

The reformers, reacting to the Protestant-Catholic dispute, rejected the deutrocanonical books. Martin Luther's translation of 1534 labeled these books as "apocrypha: not held equal to Sacred Scripture." Most modern translations now include these books at the back, no longer labeling them "apocrypha" but "deuterocanonical."

The New Testament

Following the death of Jesus, stories about His life and ministry were passed among Christians by oral tradition. There was no thought at the time of a Christian Scripture; Scripture referred to the Old Testament (a name not then in use). As the distance from Jesus grew longer, it was felt necessary to put these oral traditions on paper to preserve them to edify new Christians who had not known Jesus and to preserve the message of Jesus for future generations. Scholars now hold that the Gospel of Mark came first, c. A.D. 65 (although some place it earlier); Matthew and Luke, c. 65; and John, c. 95. Besides these Gospels, there were letters from Paul and other Apostles written to the early churches — letters which formulated Church teaching and doctrine. Luke wrote an early history of the Church which we know as the Acts of the Apostles. These works were circulated to instruct members of the Church and to make new converts. In addition, other written material was appearing, some associated with the heresies of the early ages, works now referred to as Christian apocrypha.

When the Church passed from the apostolic era to the era of the Church Fathers, the Fathers themselves began quoting from these works in establishing doctrine and discipline for the new Church, giving them the status of sacredness. St. Polycarp (c. 69-155), a disciple of St. John, mentions eighteen of the books now accepted. St. Ignatius (d. 107), said to have been consecrated by St. Peter, mentions twenty-four of the books in the seven letters from him that are still extant. By A.D. 200 there was general acceptance of the Gospels, the Pauline epistles, Acts, 1 Peter and 1 John. By the end of the fourth century in both Latin and Greek Churches the twenty-seven-book canon that we now have was accepted. For Catholics, the matter was solemnly defined as an article of belief by the Council of Trent in 1546. The earliest lists were approved by local councils and synods.

The Council of Hippo (393) and the Third Council of Carthage (397) each approved the list that was ultimately sanctioned by Trent. The Protestant reformers accepted the Catholic listing, although Luther in his translation believed the books of the New Testament should be graded, giving secondary rank to books he placed at the end: Hebrews, James, Jude, and Revelation.

Inspiration

The Bible is the inspired word of God. It was written down under the guidance of the Holy Spirit and it is without error. As St. Paul tells us: "All scripture is given by the inspiration of God" (2 Tim 3:16). Hence, the entire Bible is true, trustworthy and dependable — even in matters not directly related to doctrine or salvation. Some biblical fundamentalists go even further and affirm that God dictated the Bible word for word as an author would to a secretary.

Inspiration has been defined thusly: "A supernatural impulse by means of which the Holy Spirit excited and moved the sacred writers to write and helped them when they wrote in such a way that they could conceive exactly, wished to report faithfully, and expressed with infallible accuracy all that God commanded them to write and nothing else" (Pope Leo XIII, encyclical on Scripture). Thus God and the human writers are both true authors of the Scriptures. God did not dictate the Bible word for word and have the author record it like a robot, but God inspired the author to communicate His message in the way God wanted it conveyed by the human writer. God did not remove the free will of the author but so worked in harmony with the writer that often he was unaware of the working of the Holy Spirit, causing the human author to will himself to write and accomplish what God willed. The inspiration God gave was direct and detailed. It was not a vague inspiration such as a poet gets when he or she sees something beautiful and is inspired to write a poem. Also, the sacred writer brought his own personality, skill, and knowledge to the work.

It should be noted that God's inspiration was limited to the original text, not to copies and translations of the original book. The aim of biblical scholarship is to make the texts we have today as close as possible to the original text.

It is also the task of biblical interpreters to determine the method God chose to speak to us and to determine the message God wished to convey through the human author, and therein we come to a serious problem of modern Scripture.

Interpretation

The Bible is understood by readers through the marvelous operation of the Holy Spirit, who illuminates the believer and quickens the Word to him as He empowers the believer to discern and interpret.

This fundamentalist statement makes every reader of the Bible his own interpreter, although in some of the fundamentalist groups, this power is centered in the group leader.

This matter of private judgment in interpreting Sacred Scripture is one of the distinguishing marks of Protestantism, wherein each person bases his or her religious practice on the meaning that individual personally draws from Scripture. One of the results of this teaching is the fractionalization of Protestantism into so many different religious bodies and sects, the founder of each such body basing his or her divergence from other Protestant bodies on his or her different interpretation of Scripture. These interpreters believe they are guided by the Holy Spirit, but since they come up with different interpretations, this conclusion has to be false, since God does not contradict Himself.

The fact is that few Protestants or Catholics are equipped for a scientific interpretation of the Bible, and it is a highly specialized science called hermeneutics. Raymond E. Brown, a recognized scholar, has written: "The Greek word *hermeneia* was used to cover a broad scope in the process of clarification. First, it could refer to interpretation by *speech* itself, inasmuch as language interprets what is in a man's mind; this usage of the word was especially significant when there was an instance of human language used to interpret divine will. Second, the word *hermeneia* could refer to the process of *translation* from an unintelligible language to an intelligible one, e.g., the *hermeneia* of tongues in 1 Cor 12:10, which was a charismatic gift with a revelatory character. . . . Third, the word *hermeneia* was used for *interpretation by commentary and explanation.*"

Hermeneutics is a science by which rules are formulated for determining and explaining the true sense of Scripture. Study is made of the history and culture of the people of the time, the sacred writer, the literary character of the writing, the vocabulary, the translation against the original or the oldest existing texts, and so on. Preparation for such a science takes many years of training. Even so, highly trained and specialized scholars will differ among themselves on interpretation, as any good biblical commentary will quickly demonstrate. Is there no way, then, that we can be certain of the intention of the original author? What did he intend his word to convey? What did God have in mind in giving inspiration to the author? Is there no way in which we can know where truth lies? Someone may say that is what the Holy Spirit does in inspiring the correct answer. But how do we know the Holy Spirit is operative in any particular case? If two expert scholars contradict each other over the interpretation of a particular text, in which one is the Holy Spirit guiding or could it be in neither? Pointedly, what is being asked here is: Did God after giving us His inspired word, give us no way to be sure of what that word meant? Is there no means of certainty as to God's plan of salvation for all of us? In short, did

God give us the Sacred Scriptures and then leave us to our own imperfect devices to rationalize what He meant?

The answer is no, He did not. Scripture presents God to us as a loving, caring, and concerned Father, one who does not abandon His children. In ancient days He spoke to His people through the prophets. When the Old Covenant came to fulfillment God gave humanity a new means of access to Himself through Christ, the Word made flesh. When it came time for Christ to be reunited with the Father, Jesus did not leave His followers orphans but gave them two means to know His and the Father's mind — the Church and Tradition — two words that are a red flag for many who have been conditioned by the propaganda of the time.

3

Tradition

The Bible has been officially endorsed by the Catholic church as the inspired, infallible Word of God. Then an adulterant is allowed to intrude, which is, in fact, *the basis for all Roman Catholic error*! This is *tradition*!

The Catholic Church's teaching on Tradition is one of its most misunderstood doctrines and the focus for attack against the legitimacy of the Catholic Faith. Let it be said at the very outset that it is also Catholic teaching that nothing in Tradition can contradict the Bible, for biblical contradiction could not be part of Catholic belief. Jesus warned of false tradition (Mt 15:6) when He condemned the Pharisees. St. Paul warned against human traditions which were not those of Christ (Col 2:8). But at the same time he recognized true tradition (2 Thes 3:6) which he himself was passing on to his converts. Also in the same Epistle he writes (2 Thes 2:15):

"So then, brethren, stand firm and hold to the traditions which you were taught by us, either by word of mouth or by letter."

The above quotation is important because it shows that history and teaching were passed on also by word of mouth. Not everything the Apostles taught was put into writing. Tradition existed before the New Testament was written. The Gospel of Luke, for example, is a Gospel of tradition. Luke did not know

Jesus but gathered the stories he had been told about Jesus and saved them for posterity by writing his Gospel. No scholar would hold that Luke wrote everything that existed about Jesus in the early Church (as the Gospel of John shows). Likewise for the teaching of the Apostles, both written and oral. Paul wrote the doctrine of the Church, but the teaching of a few other Apostles exists only in short epistles. We have to turn to post-apostolic writings, first to the Fathers who knew the Apostles, and then to their successors, who inherited the traditions they passed down, and to other contemporary writings, such as the *Didache*, which in turn have to be sifted and compared.

. The word "tradition" comes from the Latin *tradere*, meaning to transmit or to hand on. People who do not know Catholic teaching become upset with the word because they believe it conflicts with Scripture, but this is not possible unless Christ and the Apostles could contradict themselves. In any discussion of the word at the outset a distinction must be made between Tradition (capital T) and tradition (small t). Sacred Tradition is the body of the teachings of Christ and His Apostles which are not explicitly contained in the Bible but passed on by Jesus to His Apostles, who in turn passed on these teachings to succeeding generations. Catholics also use the word (small t) to mean some action or something that has been customary in the Church for a long time. The *Catholic Commentary on Holy Scripture* puts it this way: "Tradition does not add anything to the Scriptures considered as God's Word, no more than man's spirit adds anything to his body. Spirit and body, or flesh, are two distinct, irreducible, but correlative aspects of the one reality, man. Similarly, Tradition and Scripture are but two aspects of the one entity, God's Word. To attempt the interpretation of Scripture without recourse to tradition would be like performing a surgical operation on a corpse."

Let me give a parallel example. The United States Constitution is not a long document — seven articles and twenty-six amendments. Yet the constant work of the Supreme Court over two centuries has been to interpret this document. In order to do so, the justices must go beyond the document to discover what was in the minds of the founding fathers who drew up the Constitution. This is done through letters and writings of these same fathers. James Madison, one of the framers, set himself a staggering task as he wrote "losing not a moment unnecessarily between adjournment and reassembling of the Convention, I was able to write out my daily notes during the session or within a few days after its close." Madison did not miss a single session, and anyone interpreting the Constitution and its Bill of Rights should necessarily study Madison's record of what went on and why. Similarly, anyone interpreting the Scriptures should try to find out what oral teaching the Apostles passed on to their successors, the Fathers of the Church, to whom they gave "their own position of teaching authority" (St. Irenaeus, *Adv. Haer.*).

One of the courses every Catholic seminarian must take on the way to the priesthood is Patristics (the study of the Church Fathers). It was the Fathers who inherited the teaching of the Apostles. It was the Fathers who set the list of what books were to be considered Sacred Scripture. It was the Fathers who composed the basic profession of faith — the Creed, or statement of beliefs necessary to be called a Christian. It was the Fathers who developed the first forms of worship which have developed into present liturgies. It was the Fathers who in stating doctrine and refuting heresies began the science we know today as Theology.

As a recent document from the Holy See (*Instruction on the Fathers of the Church in the Formation of Priests*) points out: "The Fathers are thus witnesses and guarantors of an authentic Catholic Tradition, and hence their authority in theological questions has been very great and always remains so. When it has been necessary to denounce the deviation of certain schools of thought, the Church has always referred to the Fathers as a guarantee of truth. Various Councils, for instance the Councils of Chalcedon and Trent, begin their solemn declarations with reference to the patristic Tradition by using the formula: 'In following the Holy Fathers . . . etc.' "

That the Fathers were intended to be keepers of this doctrine can be seen in the words of Paul to Timothy (2 Tim 2:2): "What you have heard from me before many witnesses entrust to faithful men who will be able to teach others." This apostolic teaching which was to be passed on from generation to generation is the Tradition of which we speak. This oral truth which was passed on is free from error because of the promise of Christ to His Apostles. Jesus told His Apostles that even though He was departing the world, He would be in them (Jn 14:23). He would send these followers the Holy Spirit who "will teach you all things and bring to your remembrance all that I have said to you" (14:26). This presence of Christ and the Holy Spirit would be present in His Church for all time (Mt 28:20), keeping it from error in the matter of faith and morals.

To summarize Tradition, Vatican Council II had this to say in 1965: "Sacred Tradition and Sacred Scripture, then, are bound closely together, and communicate one with the other. For both of them, flowing out from the same divine well-spring, come together in some fashion to form one thing, and move toward the same goal. Sacred Scripture is the speech of God as it is put down in writing under the breath of the Holy Spirit, and Tradition transmits in its entirety the Word of God which has been entrusted to the Apostles by Christ the Lord and the Holy Spirit. It transmits it to the successors of the Apostles so that, enlightened by the Spirit of truth, they may faithfully preserve, expound, and spread it abroad by their preaching. Thus it comes about that the Church does not draw her certainty about all revealed truths from the holy Scriptures alone. Hence, both Scripture and Tradition must be accepted and honored with equal feelings of reverence and devotion.

"Sacred Scripture and Sacred Tradition make up a single

sacred deposit of the Word of God which is entrusted to the Church. By adhering to it the entire holy people united to its pastors, remains always faithful to the teachings of the Apostles, to the brotherhood, to the breaking of the bread and the prayers (cf. Acts 2:42). So, in maintaining, practicing, and professing the faith that has been handed on there should be a remarkable harmony between the bishops and the faithful" (*Dogmatic Constitution on Divine Revelation* 9,10).

Finally, something should be said on traditions (small t) in the Church. These are things and actions that have been long customary and accepted by the People of God. This type of tradition has often been confused with Tradition by people unfamiliar with Catholic doctrine and practice. Every nation and family has its traditions — the handing down of beliefs, information, and customs from one generation to the next — so too the Church. For example, the Council of Trent (1545-63) decreed a new manner for the celebration of the Mass (the Eucharist). While the essence of the Mass is unchangeable, since it comes from Christ, the words and actions surrounding that action can be changed. This new method of saying Mass became a tradition in the Church and over the centuries became venerable and holy. However, at Vatican Council II, held the early 1960s, the world's bishops set about updating the Church, yet at the same time returning it closer to its apostolic roots. Among the changes ordered were those in liturgical practice. The new Mass liturgy that came out of the Council upset some people who wanted to stay with the old tradition, and even a few went into schism over the changes, making the same mistake as many fundamentalists by confusing Tradition with man-made traditions.

The Council also changed other accidentals of past cultural expression. For example, the sacrament instituted by Christ and recommended in the Letter of James (5:14) was known as the Sacrament of Extreme Unction and popularly called the Last

Rites. The Council decreed that it should be revised to bring out more clearly its apostolic meaning, and its name was changed back to Anointing of the Sick. Thus a tradition was changed to make it more conformable to Tradition.

Thus it should be evident to everyone but those with closed minds that Tradition and tradition are two very different things.

4

The Church

The contention that our Lord Jesus Christ established the Roman Catholic church as it exists today is a total fabrication. There was no such thing as a Roman Catholic church during the first three hundred years after the Lord's ascension. Catholics are not Christians. Their church is the whore of Babylon. There is no salvation in the Roman Catholic church.

The Church is God's presence in salvation history. It began when sin destroyed communion with God and God called humanity to repentance. The embryonic Church was present in prehistory, and its public history began with the calling of Abraham to be the father of a great nation. God's presence was seen in Israel, to whom prophets spoke God's message and prepared them for what was to come. "The days are coming, says the Lord, when I will make a new covenant with the house of Israel and the house of Judah. It will not be like the covenant I made with their fathers the day I took them by the hand and led them forth from the land of Egypt" (Jer 31:31-32). This theme of a new covenant was a constant theme of the prophets. The promise would come to fruition in Jesus and be sealed in His blood (Lk 22:20). Jesus told His followers that He had not come to destroy the Old Law but to fulfill it, to build on what was already there (Mt 5:17). Jesus announced a new covenant to which all the people of the world would be invited (Mt 28:19-20). To begin this work, Jesus called twelve from among His followers, representing the twelve tribes of Israel. The Twelve were to be the foundation stones of the New Jerusalem. Jesus chose one of the Twelve, Peter, to be the leader of His visible Church (Mt 16:18). It was a Church which had unity (Jn 10:16), so that there would be one flock and one shepherd. Jesus would be with this Church always to the end of time (Mt 28:20). The Father will send the Holy Spirit to this Church to keep it faithful to the teachings of Jesus (Jn 14:26), and the Holy Spirit will guide the Church to all truth (Jn 16:13). The Church is a sheepfold, and entrance into it is through Jesus, the gate (Jn 10:1-10).

The visible Church Jesus founded and left behind as His inheritance to all peoples could be identified by four marks: one, holy, catholic, and apostolic.

One. It was the will of Jesus that there be one single Church, not a multiplicity of churches, and that this Church would have a unity (oneness) of its own. On the night before His death, Jesus prayed for His Church: "that they may all be one; even as thou, Father, art in me, and I in thee, that they may also be in us, so that the world may believe that thou hast sent them" (Jn 17:21). St. Paul saw the Church as the Mystical Body of Christ: Jesus as the vine and the faithful of the Church its branches. This oneness and unity became essential. He wrote: "There is one body and one Spirit, just as you were called to the one hope that belongs to your call, one Lord, one faith, one baptism, one God and Father of us all, who is above all and through all and in all" (Eph 4:4-5).

Thus every division within the Church, every breakaway, is contrary to the will of God and becomes a scandal to the non-Christian world. In divisions the unity of the Apostolic Church is fractured; in His Church the Christians "devoted themselves to the apostles' teaching and fellowship, to the breaking of the bread and the prayers" (Acts 2:42), a unity in faith, love, and worship under the guidance of the Apostles. Unity, however, is not to be equated with uniformity. The Church was to draw men and women from all races, languages, and cultures, and because of this there would be variations in liturgical expression, modes of prayer, church adornment and so on. But these varied modes of expression were accidentals, while the essential unity of the Church remained. Paul had this diversity in mind when he described himself as being all things to all men (See 1 Cor 9:19-23).

Holy. Since Jesus Christ is holy, and one with His Church in the Mystical Body (Jn 15:5), it follows that His Church must be holy. This does not mean that individual members cannot fail Him, just as there was failure in the original apostolic body. God forces no person's free will. There have been bad popes and bad priests, bad laymen and bad ministers, but the Church as Church is holy. Peter told the early Christians what they were: "You are a chosen race, a royal priesthood, a holy nation, God's own people" (1 Pt 2:9).

As *The Church's Confession of Faith* puts it: "When Holy Scripture speaks of 'holiness,' it does not primarily mean ethical perfection, but rather *being singled out from the domain of the worldly and belonging to God.* Christians and the Church do indeed live in the world, but they are not part of it (Jn 17:11,14-15). The Church is holy because she comes from God and is ordained to Him. She is holy because the holy God, the One who is different from the whole world, keeps faith with her unconditionally and does not abandon her to the powers of death or the transitoriness of the world (Mt 16:18). The Church is holy because Jesus Christ is indissolubly linked to her (Mt 28:20), because the powerful presence of the Holy Spirit is permanently promised to her (Jn 14:26; 16:7-9). She is holy because the goods of salvation have been permanently given to her and entrusted to her for transmission — these are the truths of faith, the sacraments of new life, ministries and offices."

From the earliest days of the Church, down through history, there have been those who have lived the holiness expected of all Christians. Those whose lives have been examined and

33

proven are called saints and held up as models for what Christian life should be. They are believable proof to the holiness to which the Church calls all its members. At the same time there have been and are sinners within the Church. The Church, knowing Christ gave His life as an expiation for sin, calls sinners to penance and reformation, just as a loving mother clasps sinners to her bosom, helping them to atone for their failures and reminding them that they are called to a life of sanctification. The constant call of the Church is renewal of Christian life in the spirit of the Gospels and thus giving witness to holiness.

Catholic. The word "Catholic" was coined by one of the early Fathers of the Church, Ignatius of Antioch (died c. 107), who reputedly was a disciple of St. John and made bishop of Antioch by St. Peter. He applied (*Letter to the Smyrnians*) the term to the Church to signify its universal mission to all peoples of all time to come and to the universality of its doctrine. It is a Greek word (*katholikos*) meaning "universal." God is catholic because He is everywhere and the ultimate creator of all things. Jesus Christ is catholic because He is God and His mission was the salvation of all people. As one writer puts it, ' "The Church is catholic' means that she proclaims the whole faith and the whole of salvation for the whole man and the whole of mankind. Every truth of salvation and every means of salvation has its home in her." By God's will all people are called to this Catholic unity.

1. The Church is catholic because it fulfills the great command of Christ to carry the Gospel to all people (Mt 28:19-20) in every age and for all time.

2. The Church is catholic because it unites the Churches founded by the Apostles into one global whole. These Churches, while having their own discipline and liturgical life, their own languages and customs, are united in one body of faith, in one sacramental life, and in one unified and collegiate and undivided structure.

As with oneness, catholicity does not mean uniformity. It

does mean that these diverse Churches are united in the same universal communion. In short, as *The Teaching of Christ* says, "The Church is universal, or catholic, in that it continues to teach all of what Christ taught. And it regards itself as obliged by Christ to teach that doctrine to all men."

Apostolic. The final mark of the true Christian Church is that it is apostolic. "It is the same community as the Church of the apostolic age," is the way *The Teaching of Christ* puts it. Since Christ promised that His Church would endure until the end of time and that He would be with it always, the Church, founded by the Apostles, had to have apostolic continuity, teaching always what the Apostles taught. Thus, for example, the Church today is criticized for holding abortion to be wrong and sinful. Yet this is a teaching from the earliest times. In the *Didache* or *Teaching of the Twelve Apostles*, a manuscript which has been dated to the first century, although some think it was later (but whether first or second century it was the teaching of the early Church), we read the command: "Do not kill a fetus by abortion or commit infanticide." It is as applicable today as when given to the infant Church.

Besides being apostolic in teaching, the Church must be apostolic in succession. The Apostles, in order that the mission confided to them by Christ would continue after their deaths, appointed collaborators to continue and consolidate the work they had begun. They also ruled, as St. Clement of Rome (d. c. 97) tells us in his Letter to the Corinthians, that, upon the death of these successors and collaborators, other proven men should be appointed to succeed them. Thus a continuous hierarchy was established to continue the work of the Twelve. These men were given the Greek name *episkopos*, literally overseer, which in English we term "bishop."

When the Reformation came, the newly-formed Protestant churches broke away from the Catholic Church and thus lost this apostolic succession. It remained for a time in the Anglican

Church, but when Michael Parker became head of the Anglican hierarchy in 1559, this succession was broken because a new rite for ordination was substantially defective both in form and content. Not all who went into schism from the Catholic Church lost apostolic succession — the Old Catholic and the Orthodox Churches still possess it.

Apostolic succession also comes through the successors of Peter, whom Christ renamed the rock on which He would build His Church. He also commanded Peter to strengthen his brothers, and in His last meeting with Peter after the resurrection, as recorded in John, Jesus bade Peter, "Tend my sheep." These successors to Peter were called popes (from Greek *pappas*, a familiar title for "father"). Peter's third successor was St. Clement of Rome, mentioned above, who governed from Rome A.D. 88-97. His *Letter to the Corinthians* is an important historical document. In it he rebukes the Corinthians for a schism that had broken out among them. Its historical importance is that it shows the Bishop of Rome intervening authoritatively in the affairs of another Church to settle a dispute and indicates the primacy that was given to a successor of St. Peter.

For the first three centuries the Roman Catholic church did not exist. The Roman church came into being about A.D. 325. The great standard-bearers of early Christian truth (St. Clement, St. Ignatius, St. Polycarp, St. Irenaeus, St. Gregory) were not Roman Catholic in faith.

It is a fact that many who do not like the Catholic Church insist on calling it the Roman Catholic Church. Jimmy Swaggart when he writes the term even refuses to capitalize the word Church, although one does not know what this proves other than his own prejudice. Although the Catholic Church has its seat of government in Rome, it is far broader than just the Latin Rite

36

Church which is also headquartered there. The Catholic Church includes many diverse liturgies and liturgical languages, all of which have the same doctrine, roots, and governance under the pope. These rites are the following.

Alexandrian Rite (Liturgy of St. Mark): COPTS: Egypt and Near East; ETHIOPIANS: Ethiopia and Somalia.

Antiochene Rite (Liturgy of St. James of Jerusalem): MALANKARESE (Syriac): India; MARONITES (Syriac and Arabic): Lebanon, Syria, Egypt and diaspora; SYRIANS (Syriac, Arabic): Lebanon, Iraq, Egypt, Syria and diaspora.

Armenian Rite (Greek Liturgy of St. Basil): Near East, Europe, Africa, Americas.

Chaldean Rite (derived from Antiochene Rite): CHALDEANS (Syriac and Arabic): Egypt, Iraq, Iran, Lebanon, Syria, Turkey, United States. SYRO-MALABARESE (Syrian and Malayan): India (mostly Malabar region).

Byzantine Rite (Rite of St. James of Jerusalem, reformed by St. Basil and others): ALBANIANS (Albanian): Albania; BULGARIANS (Old Slavonic): Bulgaria; BYELORUSSIANS (White Russians) (Old Slavonic): Europe, America, Australia; GEORGIANS (Georgian): Southern Russia, France; Greeks (Greek): Greece, Asia Minor, Europe; HUNGARIANS (Greek, Hungarian, English): Hungary, Americas; ITALO-ALBANIANS (Greek, Italo-Albanian): Italy, Americas; GREEK CATHOLICS-MELKITES (Greek, Arabic, Portugese, Spanish):Syria, Lebanon, Jordan, Israel, United States, Brazil, Canada, Australia, Mexico; ROMANIANS (Romanian): Romania, United States; RUSSIANS (Old Slavonic): Russia, Americas, Europe, Australia, China; RUTHENIANS (Old Slavonic, English): Hungary, Czechoslovakia, Americas, Australia; SLOVAKS (Old Slavonic): Czechoslovakia, Canada; UKRANIANS (Old Slavonic, Ukranian): Russia and Europe, Galicia, Poland, Americas, England, Germany, France, Australia; YUGOSLAVS, SERBS and CROATIANS (Old Slavonic): Yugoslavia.

Latin Rite (Latin and vernacular languages): Worldwide. Variations are permitted in the Latin ritual for the Toledo Rite, Dominican Rite, Tridentine Rite.

These, then, are the elements that make up the Catholic Church. All are traced back to apostolic origin. In this assemblage of so wide a variety of liturgical rituals and languages, the title Roman Catholic Church is a misnomer. More correct would be Apostolic Catholic Church; however, this title is not used except as a descriptive.

> **There is absolutely no mention of priests in the New Testament. Any person of average intelligence who is even superficially conversant with the New Testament knows that no ordered hierarchial system is even suggested within Scripture.**

The frequently heard fundamentalist charge that the Catholic Church did not exist before 325 is historically absurd. The structure of the Church was organized by the Apostles. In the beginning the Apostles themselves were the rulers of the new community of believers. As the Palestinian church grew, the Apostles felt the need for helpers (Acts 6) and they ordained (laid hands on) seven men who were called deacons and who were directed to a ministry of service. As the Church spread beyond Palestine and new communities developed, the Apostles, who were traveling evangelists, left behind overseers (bishops) to govern these new communities and celebrate the Eucharist (the breaking of the bread). These bishops were ordained by the Apostles. In time these new communities also grew and the bishop in turn ordained priests (*presbyteros*) to assist him.

To say these developments are not substantiated by Scripture shows a very selective use of Scripture. The first ordained order of *deacons* is described in Acts 6. St. Paul (who died in A.D. 65) in his first letter to Timothy (Chapter 3) describes the qualities a man should have to become a *bishop*. In his Letter to Titus, whom Paul had ordained Bishop of Crete, the Apostle to the Gentiles writes (1:5): "This is why I left you in Crete, that you might amend what was defective and appoint elders [*presbyters* (Greek for priests)] in every town as I directed you." Paul then gives the qualifications a man needs to be a priest and follows this up with a discussion of bishops.

Therefore, it is quite evident from Scripture that within three decades of the death of Christ the Church was already hierarchically organized: Into a head (Peter), Apostles, bishops, priests, deacons.

With the exception of Apostles, whose role as these chosen by Christ ceased at their deaths, the hierarchy of the early Church is the same as the ordained hierarchy of the Catholic Church today. Thus apostolic succession is maintained through the popes, who are successors to Peter; the bishops, successors to the Apostles; the priests, successors to those early priests; and the deacons. If the Church is to endure to the end of time, it is only good sense that the Apostles would organize their Church so that it could be governed effectively and could endure to the end of time, as Christ promised (Mt 18:20).

Why do some people assert that the Catholic Church did not appear until around A.D. 325? The answer is found in a mistaken knowledge of history. When the persecution of the Church began under Nero, and Sts. Peter and Paul lost their lives to Christian hatred, the Church became an underground Church — the Church of the Catacombs, the underground burial places where Christians met in secret. Peter's successor, Pope St. Linus (d. 76) became a martyr. His successor, Pope St. Anacletus (also known by his Latin name of Cletus) died in the persecution of Diocletian. He had been ordained a priest by St. Peter. The third successor of St. Peter was Pope St. Clement, whose Roman home still exists beneath the basilica which bears his name. He was exiled to the Crimea by Trajan, labored in a mine, and was thrown into the sea c. A.D. 97. And so on down the list of the early popes.

Change came to the proscribed religion under the Emperor Constantine, whose mother, St. Helena, was a Christian and who himself was sympathetic to Christianity before he came to power. In the battle which won him the throne his troops fought under the banner of the Cross. In 313 Constantine signed the Edict of Milan, making Christianity a lawful religion, and allowed it to emerge from the catacombs. Constantine also presented Pope Melchiades with the Lateran Palace for an official residence. The estate had once belonged to Plautius Lateranus but had been confiscated for the state by Nero. The Lateran Basilica became the pope's church, and it is still the Cathedral of Rome, the official church of the pope (not St. Peter's Basilica as so many think). This emergence of the Church from the catacombs is what some fundamentalists think is the beginning of the Catholic Church, but it was already there, before and after the time of Nero.

The reasoning presented above is bare bones because of the nature of this book. Readers wishing more detailed explanations will find them in books listed in the bibliography at the end of this volume.

5

The Papacy

The Holy Word of God never shows that Jesus ordained one man to be above all others in the Church. We know that Christ is the head of the Church. Peter was never the head of the Church, nor any man. Moreover, there is no historical record that Peter was ever even in Rome.

At the outset let it be stated that Jesus Christ is the head of the Church, but since the Church exists in the world, it needs some one to care for its daily affairs. This is the person called the pope, a word which is not in his official title. The word pope comes from the Greek *pappas*, which literally means papa and which became the popular and familiar name for the Bishop of Rome. The actual title for the pope is: Bishop of Rome, Vicar of Jesus Christ, Successor of the Prince of the Apostles, Supreme Pontiff of the Universal Church, Patriarch of the West, Primate of Italy, Archbishop and Metropolitan of the Province of Rome, Sovereign of the State of Vatican City, Servant of the Servants of God. While the pope governs the Church on earth, he does so as vicar of Jesus Christ. The word vicar means one serving as a substitute, a stand-in for another, or as generally used, an administrative deputy. Moreover, the Church in Catholic teaching embraces both the living and the dead (those who will find salvation). The pope's task is the care and governance of the Church on earth, of which Christ is the true head.

Fundamentalists have difficulty with the papacy because of two beliefs: 1) that Peter was never appointed head of the Church by Jesus Christ; and 2) that Peter was never in Rome.

Who Was Peter?

The Gospels were written to tell of the Good News of Jesus Christ, and consequently He is the central figure. But after Jesus, the one about whom the Gospels is most concerned is Peter. We first meet Peter in the Gospels when he accompanied his brother Andrew to the Jordan River where John was baptizing. Andrew was standing with the Baptist when Jesus went by. John pointed Jesus out to Andrew, saying: "Behold, the Lamb of God." Andrew left John to follow after Jesus, who invited him to come to His lodgings. Andrew was so impressed with Jesus that he immediately went looking for his brother, Simon. When he found him, Andrew told Simon, "We have found the Messiah," and took his brother to the Master. When Simon appeared before Jesus, the Lord looked at him and said: "So you are Simon, the son of John? You shall be called Cephas (which means Peter)" (Jn 1:35-42). Cephas is the Greek word for rock. Actually, since Christ spoke Aramaic, He used the Aramaic word for rock — *Kepha*, which the Gospels translated into Greek.

Peter and Andrew returned to their home on the Sea of Galilee, where they had a fishing business. Not long afterwards, Jesus arrived there and found Peter and Andrew preparing to fish. "He called out to them: 'Follow me and I will make you become fishers of men.'" Peter and Andrew left their business to their father and some hired employees and followed Jesus. That night Jesus stayed in Peter's home, where He found Peter's mother-in-law ill and He cured her. Thus Peter and Andrew were the first Apostles chosen by Jesus, and from that moment on Peter becomes prominent in the Gospels.

When the Twelve are finally assembled, it is Peter who always heads the list when it is mentioned. The Gospels also picture Peter as spokesman for the Twelve (e.g, Jn 6:68, Mk 8:29, etc.).

It is Peter who attempts to walk on the water to reach Jesus, and it is Peter whom Jesus sends to get the coin to pay for the Temple tax. It is Peter who wants to erect a memorial to the Transfiguration of Jesus. He is also the first to declare Jesus the Messiah. Jesus foresaw that Peter would fail Him after His arrest and warned Peter that Satan was seeking him. Jesus was to tell Peter that the Apostle would deny Jesus three times. But Jesus also foresaw Peter's repentance and told him, "When you have returned again, strengthen your brothers." Strengthening the brothers was the work of a leader. After the resurrection Peter and John hasten to the tomb. John arrives first and then waits for Peter to catch up so that Peter can be the first to enter. St. Paul tells us (1 Cor 15:5) that after the resurrection Jesus appeared first to Peter and then to the other Apostles.

In the Book of Acts, which is the history of the very early Church and then in its later chapters focuses on the missions of Paul, Peter is again the leader. It is he who calls for the election of a replacement for Judas. It is Peter who delivers the Pentecost sermon that results in the baptism of about three thousand. Peter works the first miracle in Acts (Acts 3) and then addresses the people.

When Peter and John are arrested because of the miracle, it is Peter who defends their faith in Jesus before the Sanhedrin.

To Peter was given God's desire that the mission of salvation should include gentiles (Acts 10), and he was the first to receive gentiles into the Church. In Chapter 12 of Acts, Peter, whose leadership took him around to the various Christian communities, was arrested by Herod, who probably intended to kill him as he had killed James, the brother of John, but Peter was rescued by an angel. After this incident Luke turns the focus of Acts upon his mentor, Paul, and for Peter's ensuing career we have to depend upon Church Tradition.

43

Peter as Head of the Church

There are two incidents in the Gospels concerning Peter on which Catholic Tradition has placed great emphasis.

The first incident is recorded in Matthew 16:13-19. Jesus and His Apostles were at the foot of Mt. Hermon, near where Herod the Great had built a temple to Caesar Augustus. Jesus asks His Apostles whom they think He is. Peter replies for the group: "You are the Christ [the Messiah], Son of the living God." Matthew goes on:

> "And Jesus answered him, 'Blessed are you, Simon Bar-Jona! For flesh and blood has not revealed this to you, but my Father who is in heaven. And I tell you, you are Peter and on this rock I will build my church, and the powers of death shall not prevail against it. I will give you the keys of the kingdom of heaven, and whatever you bind on earth shall be bound in heaven, and whatever you loose upon earth shall be loosed in heaven.' "

Catholic Tradition has always interpreted these verses to mean: 1) that Jesus was founding a visible Church that would exist in the world and that it would last to the end of time (see also Mt 28:20); 2) that Peter would be the foundation stone of this Church in the world and its first leader.

Fundamentalists, of course, deny this interpretation, for not to do so would undermine their other interpretations of the Bible. Jimmy Swaggart in his diatribe against Catholics tries to prove this point with a semantic argument: "In the original biblical text different words are used for 'Peter' and 'rock.' 'Peter' is petros, referring to 'a pebble or small stone,' while 'rock' is petra, which designates 'a stone cliff or a huge boulder.' " Unfortunately, all Swaggart is doing is revealing that he knows nothing about Greek semantics. Greek and Latin nouns, pronouns, and adjectives are declined into cases which are indicated by different endings at the end of the word indicating its relationship to other words. Petros and petra mean the exactly same thing, rock, except that petra has a different ending to show its relationship to the preposition "on." However, this argument is silly to begin with, because Jesus did not speak Greek but Aramaic and the word for "rock" in Aramaic is *kepha*, so the verse in Aramaic would be rendered: "you are Kepha and on this kepha I will build my Church."

The second passage related to Peter that the Church holds of utmost importance is John 21:15-19. It is John's last recorded conversation of the Lord and it is with Peter. Seven of the Apostles were fishing on the Sea of Galillee. Jesus appeared on the shore and the Apostles came ashore and had breakfast with Him. John continues the account:

> *"When they had finished breakfast, Jesus said to Simon Peter, 'Simon, son of John, do you love me more than these?' He said to Him, 'Yes, Lord; you know that I love you.' . . . A second time he said to him, 'Simon, son of John, do you love me?' He said to him,'Yes, Lord; you know that I love you.' He said to him, 'Tend my sheep.' He said to him the third time, ' . . . Do you love me?' Peter was grieved because he said to him the third time, 'Do you love me?' And he said to him, 'Lord, you know everything; you know that I love you.' Jesus said to him, 'Feed my sheep. Truly, truly, I say to you, when you were young, you girded yourself and walked where you would; but when you are old, you will stretch out your hands, and another will gird you and carry you where you do not wish to go.' (This he said to show by what death he was to glorify God.) And after this he said to him, 'Follow me.'"*

Catholic Tradition teaches that in this conversation, Jesus was confirming Peter as head of His Church, commanding him to see that Christians were fed the doctrine He had taught, and prophesying that Peter would be put to death for the Faith. John does not tell us how Peter died because that fact was so well known to members of the Church that it did not need repeating. Tradition also tells that after preaching the Faith in Palestine, Peter then went to Antioch, because it had become the center of Christianity, and ruled as bishop there until it was decided to move to Rome because it was the center of the Roman empire, which ruled so much of the known world. Tradition also tells us that Peter was arrested during Nero's persecution, crucified because he was a non-Roman, and buried near his place of crucifixion.

"But the Bible never says Peter was in Rome."

But the Bible does. While there were many things that happened connected with Jesus and the Apostles that are not written in the Bible (see Jn 21:25), Peter's presence in Rome is confirmed by it. In his first epistle Peter closes by saying, "She who is at Babylon, who is likewise chosen, sends you greetings; so does my son, Mark" (5:13). "She who is chosen" refers to the Church in Rome. "Babylon" is a Christian code word for Rome and the Roman Empire. Examine Revelation 17:5 where the author uses Babylon — mother of harlots and the earth's abomination, drunk on the blood of Christian martyrs — in this sense. At the time Peter was writing, Babylon was no longer a great city but a deserted relic of mud huts.

Babylon was conquered in 275 B.C. by the Seleucids, who built a new capital, Seleucia, to which they moved the people of Babylon, and what had been a great administrative center under Cyrus the Great, who captured it in 538 B.C., fell into decay. Other Apostles are reputed to have worked in the area of Persia, but not Peter.

The clinching argument, however, for the presence of Peter in Rome has been the discovery of his original tomb and bones, directly under the main altar of St. Peter's Basilica. The full story of this discovery is told in Nino LoBello's *Guide to the Vatican* (Chicago Review Press). LoBello, a foreign correspondent for over twenty-five years, reported from Rome for *The New York Times*. He is also the author of four books on the Vatican. A very condensed gist of his account follows.

Peter was crucified in Nero's Circus and buried on Vatican Hill.

Pilgrims came secretly to his tomb to pray, marking it in the Vatican cemetery with a graffiti symbol, one that only Christians knew, which said, "Peter is here." When Constantine recognized the Church, besides giving the Lateran estate to the pope, he also built a basilica over the tomb of Peter — the first St. Peter's Basilica. The basilica was built in such a way that its main altar would be directly over Peter's tomb. As the centuries passed this exact knowledge was lost, although Tradition held the Prince of the Apostles was buried somewhere under St. Peter's. In 1506 Pope Julius II decided to replace the old basilica, and the work on the present St. Peter's began. In designing the church, the new high altar was placed directly over the altar of the original basilica. When Pope Pius XI died in 1939, he was to be buried underneath St. Peter's with other popes. In excavating for this new tomb, workers broke through a wall and looked down on an ancient Vatican Hill necropolis, some twenty feet under the present church. Pope Pius XII was elected the new pope and was aware of this discovery. Three months after his election he ordered a search to be made to uncover Peter's tomb, and a team of archaeologists went to work. In his Christmas message at the end of 1950, the pope announced that the tomb of the Apostle Peter had been located. Bones found there had not been identified. Professor Margherita Guarducci, a professor at the University of Rome, dedicated herself to this problem, and it took her years of painstaking work, often hindered by Vatican bureaucrats. Finally, on June 26,

1968, Pope Pius's successor, Pope Paul VI, announced: "New and very patient and very accurate inquiries have been carried out. The relics of St. Peter have been identified in a manner we consider convincing." Thus, after almost three decades of scientific work, the search was ended.

Today visitors with a reason can obtain a special pass that admits one to a guided tour of the discovery. The excavations are not open to the general public for fear of damage to ancient constructions. This author made the tour by entering the excavation on the south side of St. Peter's. First, one passes through several rooms of the Constantine basilica, then through an opening in its walls to enter the necropolis. Along the alleys are the tombs of ancient Romans, many with inscriptions. One makes several turns into other alleys until a wall, called the Red Wall because of its color, is reached. One goes along this wall, and suddenly the visitor is looking into the tomb of the Prince of the Apostles, his whitened bones resting in a marble urn. It is a most impressive moment.

One last word about Peter. When Jesus gave Peter the keys to heaven, He was giving him what is recognized as a symbol of authority. But Jesus went further, giving Peter authority to bind and loose not only on earth but in heaven itself. To deny this is to deny the words of the Lord. If this does not place Peter in a category above the other Apostles, then the Scripture has no meaning. Since Christ willed a head for His Church and willed the Church to last to the end of time, He had also to will that Peter would have successors who would head that Church, and that brings us to the papacy.

The Pope

Nowhere else does anti-Catholic sentiment center as it does in the papacy. The pope has been burned in effigy, caricatured in cartoons, made the focus for all sorts of imagined Catholic plots against democracy. When the pope, along with other heads of state, sent a stone to be placed in the Washington Monument, anti-Catholics stole it under cover of darkness and threw it in the Potomac River, where it was never recovered. While in the United States priests have been killed for their Faith and churches burned, it is primarily in the pope that anti-Catholic sentiment is expressed. Today distaste for Papists may be a bit more subtle, but there are still those anti-Catholic publishers, like Jack Chick or Tony Alamo, who make a living bashing the pope and the Catholic Church.

It is not to be denied that in the almost 2,000 years of the papacy there have been evil and bad popes who were a disgrace to themselves and the Church, failed representatives of the Master they were pledged to serve. There were popes who were more political than pious, more self-seeking than saintly. There were also false popes (antipopes), who claimed the chair of Peter against its rightful occupant. But having said this, let us note that there were far more saintly and dedicated popes than there were failures. In the list of 264 popes, 77 have been canonized and declared saints after thorough investigation of their lives. Another seven are beatified, having attained the final step before sainthood. Many of these popes were martyrs, giving their lives for Jesus.

In the early fifteenth century, dissident movements, forerunners of the Protestant Reformation, appeared, led by priests like John Huss and John Wycliff. To respond to charges they were making, the Council of Florence was held. The Council went beyond the Latin Church, because attending it were bishops from the East — Greeks, Armenians, and Syrians (Jacobites). One of the acts of the council was to define the papacy as it had been held in the Church: "We likewise define that the Holy Apostolic See, and the Roman Pontiff, hold the primacy throughout the entire world; and that the Roman Pontiff is the successor of blessed Peter, the chief of the Apostles, and the true vicar of Christ, and that he is head of the entire Church, and the father and teacher of all Christians; and that full power was given to him in blessed Peter by our Lord Jesus Christ, to feed, to rule, and govern the universal Church; just as contained in the acts of ecumenical Councils and in the sacred canons."

The above definition confirms what had gone before and what would come after. "The Roman Pontiff — the successor of St. Peter as the Vicar of Christ and head of the Church on earth — has full and supreme authority over the universal Church in matters pertaining to faith and morals (teaching authority), discipline and government (jurisdictional authority). The primacy of the pope is real and supreme power. It is not merely a prerogative of honor that is, of his being regarded as the first among equals. Neither does primacy imply that the pope is just the presiding officer of the collective body of bishops. The pope is the head of the Church" (*Catholic Almanac*).

Some critics object that these ideas were not present in the Apostolic Church. Of course they weren't, except in embryo. The Church is a living organism and, like all living organisms, is subject to growth and development. The simple apostolic liturgy of the blessing of the bread and blessing of the cup has developed into today's liturgy of the Eucharist. Essentially both liturgies are the same, but accidentally they are quite different. So too with the papacy. We have already mentioned how Pope St. Clement in A.D. 96 censured Corinthian Christians, reminding them of their duty to the Church and telling them that they should "learn what He [Christ] has spoken through us."

St. Ignatius of Antioch in A.D. 110, on his way to martyrdom in Rome, wrote ahead to the Church there saying it was a credit to God, deserving of its renown, ranking first in love, "being true to Christ's law and stamped with the Father's name." A few years later the martyr-bishop Polycarp of Smyrna went to Rome to have settled the manner for dating Easter, thus acknowledging the authority of the pope. In the next century St. Cyprian of Carthage wrote from North Africa: "It is on him [Peter] that He [Jesus] builds the Church, and to him that He entrusts to feed His sheep. Although He gave power to all the Apostles, yet He founded a single chair, thus establishing by His authority the font and benchmark of the churches' oneness. . . . If a man does not hold fast to this oneness of Peter, does he imagine that he still holds the Faith? If he deserts the Chair of Peter upon whom the Church was built, does he believe that he is in the same Church?" Various regional councils about this time were also ruling on the primacy of the Roman Church. Finally, St. Ambrose (c. 380) summed it all up in the slogan: *Ubi Petrus, ibi Ecclesia* (Where Peter is, there is the Church).

And this brings us to another major bone of contention between Catholics and non-Catholics — the infallibility of the pope.

6

Infallibility

Catholics teach that both the Pope and "the Church" are infallible, that is, unable to make an error. Only God is errorless, not some human institution.

Webster's New Collegiate Dictionary defines infallible thusly:

"1: incapable of error: UNERRING; 2: not liable to mislead, deceive, or disappoint: CERTAIN; 3: incapable of error in defining doctrines touching faith and morals."

The first definition pertains only to God. The second is only relative infallibility. The third is the infallibility claimed by the Catholic Church for the pope and its bishops in union with him, and the definitional limitations of this infallibility should be noticed. Moreover, infallibility is directly bestowed on the office the pope occupies and only indirectly on the person himself.

Many people believe that the Catholic Church's claim to papal infallibility means that the pope is never wrong. This is not so. If the pope were to predict the winner of next year's Super Bowl or if it will rain on this date next year, his guess would be no better than yours or mine. Catholic claims for papal infallibility extend solely to matters of faith and morals, and then only when the pope speaks solemnly and deliberately as head of the Church (*ex cathedra*). Moreover, infallibility does not extend to any priest or bishop. However, when the body of bishops act together with the pope (as in an ecumenical council) and speak on faith and morals, then they share infallibility with the pope. Pope Paul VI, under whose direction most of Vatican

Council II was held, summarizes the teaching in this way in his *Credo of the People of God*: "We believe in the infallibility enjoyed by the Successor of St. Peter when he teaches *ex cathedra* as Pastor and Teacher of all the faithful, and which is assured also to the Episcopal Body when it exercises with him the supreme magisterium [teaching office]." On this matter, Vatican Council II gives the following reasoning: "This infallibility with which the divine Redeemer willed His Church to be endowed in defining a doctrine of faith and morals extends as far as the deposit of divine revelation, which must be religiously guarded and faithfully expounded. This is the infallibility which the Roman Pontiff, as head of the college of bishops, enjoys in virtue of his office, when, as the supreme shepherd and teacher of all the faithful, who confirms his brothers in the faith (cf. Lk 22:32), he proclaims by a definitive act some doctrine of faith and morals. Therefore his definitions, of themselves, and not from the consent of the Church, are justly styled irreformable, for they are pronounced with the assistance of the Holy Spirit, an assistance promised him in blessed Peter. Therefore they need no approval of others, nor do they allow an appeal to any other judgment. For then the Roman Pontiff is not pronouncing judgment as a private person. Rather, as the supreme teacher of the universal Church, as one in whom the charisma of the infallibility of the Church herself is individually present, he is expounding or defending a doctrine of Catholic faith."

Basically, the Church is infallible because Jesus and the Holy Spirit are infallible. This is how the reasoning goes. 1. Jesus intended to found a Church and make Peter head (Mt 16:17-19). As head of the Church Peter was to confirm his brethren (Lk 22:32) and see that they received the doctrine Jesus taught and were properly guided (Jn 21:15-17). 2. Jesus promised that he would be with the Apostles and their successors for all time (Mt 28:18), so that they would be consecrated to truth (Jn 17:19). Jesus also promised to send the Holy Spirit on the Apostles so that the Holy Spirit would guide Peter and the Apostles and make clear all that Jesus had revealed to them (Jn 14:26, Jn 15:26, etc.). 3. Since Jesus promised to be with His Church for all time, the promises made to Peter and the Apostles by necessity had to be passed on to their successors, pope and bishops. 4. This presence of Jesus and the Holy Spirit in the Church is what keeps it from error. Infallibility then is not merely a gift but a necessity, since Jesus and the Holy Spirit cannot contradict themselves.

The notion of infallibility is a very logical one. In fact it becomes a necessity. Father John O'Brien, in his book *The Faith of Millions*, tells of a Protestant bishop who in a sermon declared, "For my part I have an infallible Bible and this is the only infallibility I require." At first glance this statement is one in which most Christians would agree. This author believes the Bible to be infallible. However, as Father O'Brien points out, the statement as a whole does not stand analysis.

Father O'Brien addressed himself to the bishop in this way: "Either, my dear friend, you are infallibly certain that your interpretation of the Bible is the correct one or you are not. If you maintain that you are infallibly certain, then you claim for yourself — and you cannot very well deny the same for every other reader of the Bible — a personal infallibility which you deny only to the pope and which Catholics claim only for him. According to this view each of the hundreds of millions of readers of the Bible becomes a pope, while the only one who is not a pope is the pope himself."

What the bishop is acting on is intuition, based on his training, but not infallibility. Someone has said, somewhat tongue in cheek, "Intuition is what you know for sure without knowing for certain." The only certainty in interpreting the Bible comes from infallibility and not hunches.

An infallible Bible without an infallible interpreter is a meaningless Bible. If everybody makes his or her own interpretation, no one can be sure what is meant. Is this what God intended in giving us the Bible? Hardly. He meant it to be correctly understood in accordance with the inspiration He gave the writer, and for it to be correctly understood an infallible interpreter is needed. This becomes the task of God's chosen Church.

This then brings us to the all-important question: Which then is the Church of Jesus Christ? There are many claimants to be the Church of Jesus, teaching varied and often contradicting doctrines. Yet if one is to do the will of God and not risk one's salvation, it is a question that must be answered. A logical response to this question will be made at the end of this book.

Finally, it does violence to the will of Christ to refer to His Church as "a human institution." It is an institution that exists in this world and the next. True, it is made up of human beings, but its Founder was divine, and the assured presence of the Founder and the Holy Spirit takes it out of the realm of just a "human institution," as if it were on a par with Rotary Clubs or the YMCA. There is a branch of theology called ecclesiology which is a study of what the nature of Christ's Church should be. It is an area of studies that too, too few Christians have ever encountered.

Peter vs. Paul

The outstanding role in the early Church was taken by Paul, not Peter. If Peter was supreme pontiff, Paul would have been behind him instead of opposing him (Gal 2:11). Moreover, Paul never betrayed Jesus.

Much has been made of the dispute between Peter and Paul regarding Jewish practices and gentile converts, as recounted by Paul in his letter to the Galatians. Paul's recollection must also be read in its parallel account in Acts 15, written by Luke, a disciple of Paul. The passage in Galatians 2 is used to show that

Paul did not recognize Peter as leader of the Apostles and that Peter was not infallible. These charges are not sustainable in the total context of Scripture. Evidence shows that Paul did regard Peter as the leader of the Apostles. That is why he writes in Galatians 1:18 that after his conversion, when he was ready to begin his mission, he "went up to Jerusalem to visit Cephas and stayed with him fifteen days." He went to see Peter because Peter was the recognized head of the Church and the one Paul should consult about his mission. Other passages in Paul and in the writings of Luke, Paul's disciple, show that the Apostle of the Gentiles recognized Peter as chief of the Apostles. Even reading between the lines of the Galatians controversy with Peter, Paul tells it as one who was willing to challenge the head of the Church on a matter he (Paul) believed to be in the right. Moreover, the dispute had nothing to do with infallibility. It was not a matter of doctrine (faith and morals) but one of discipline.

Perhaps a modern example will better illustrate this point. Catholic priests take a vow of celibacy. Catholic laity who wed take a marriage vow. A priest, for proper reason, can ask Rome to dispense him from the vow of celibacy and allow him to leave the priesthood and marry. Rome grants this dispensation in special cases. On the other hand Rome will not even consider a dispensation from the marriage vow: once properly entered, the marriage must last until the death of one of the partners. At first glance this seems like discrimination, and even some Catholics question the difference. But there is an important dissimilarity. between the two.

Celibacy is a discipline of the Church. Jesus praised celibacy in those who were able to be so for the sake of the kingdom of heaven (Mt 19:12), a fact many who deem celibacy unnatural forget. Jesus chose celibacy for Himself and counseled it for others but he did not mandate it for His followers. It is a counsel given as an ideal and is meant only for those who can live a celibate life. The permanence of marriage, on the other hand, is a mandate of the Lord, who, when questioned about the marriage mandate of God he had given the Pharisees ("What therefore God has joined together, let not man put asunder"), told His disciples, "Whoever divorces his wife and marries another, commits adultery against her; and if she divorces her husband and marries another, she commits adultery" (Mk 10:9-11). That is why no pope or council can ever grant a divorce. When Henry VIII demanded a divorce from the Church, the pope refused because it was not in his power on account of the words of Christ. So Henry formed the Church of England, made himself its head and gave himself a divorce. The text that brought about this rupture between England and Catholicism is today one that many conveniently forget.

So the argument over whether Peter should eat with fellow Jews or whether gentile converts should follow some Jewish practice pertained to Church discipline and not to a matter of faith. It was not a question of infallibility. Paul's disagreement with Peter was as ephemeral as if you or I disagreed with the present pope over how he divides a diocese or changes some liturgical practice or promotes a particular devotion. These things do not pertain to the doctrines of Scripture or Tradition.

Paul's role in the early Church was outstanding. Paul, more than any one else but the Lord, stamped his imprint on the Church. He not only launched the Church into Europe but the summary of teachings he gave in his epistles is the doctrine of the Church today. Paul was uniquely chosen by the Lord to render this service, but this in no way lessened Peter's role as leader. St. Thomas Aquinas is ranked by many as the greatest theologian the Catholic Church has produced, but this never entitled him to be pope.

The accusation that Peter was not chosen to be pope because he betrayed Jesus is meanspirited and contrary to Christ's will. Paul was a persecutor of the Church, a consenter to the stoning of Stephen, yet God chose him for a particular work which he fulfilled admirably. Jesus knew what Peter would do under pressure and even warned him (Jn 13:38). When the moment of truth came, Peter's first reaction was to defend his Master (Jn 18:10) but later when he was accused of being a member of Christ's band, he yielded to personal fear and denied the Lord three times. Then reminded that Jesus had warned him of this very failure, he repented and wept bitter tears (Mt 26:75). That Jesus forgave Peter is shown by the fact that it was to Peter that the resurrected Lord first appeared before being seen by the other Apostles (1 Cor 15:5). Then shortly before His Ascension the Lord appeared to Peter and some of the other Apostles. As if to make up for the three denials, three times the Lord asks Peter if he loves Him. Three times Peter protests his love, after which the Lord reconfirms him in his role, bidding him to take care of the faithful of the Church and foretelling that Peter would give his life for Jesus (Jn 21:15-19).

Prejudice and bias are no reason before the Lord to do violence to all the scriptural texts about Peter. Peter was a loving and impetuous man, devoted but sometimes distracted, one chosen by God for a unique role in His Church, who saw more to Peter than even the Gospel writers. Paul's description of the average Christian (1 Cor 1:26-31) can well be a description of Peter.

7

The Magisterium

Catholics make prelates the equal of God. If you receive a command from one who holds the place of God you must observe it.

The teaching of Jesus was already being shaped into a body of irreformable doctrine under the Apostles. Those who were to succeed the Apostles were charged with preserving this deposit of faith and teaching it correctly and without change. Thus we read Paul instructing Timothy: "Take as a model of sound teaching what you have heard me say, in faith and love in Christ Jesus. Guard the rich deposit of faith with the help of the Holy Spirit who dwells within us" (2 Tim 1:13-14). This new teaching authority that was to succeed the Apostles was to continue down through time. The Catholic Church uses a word taken from the Latin meaning teaching authority — the magisterium. This magisterium consists of the pope, successor to Peter, and the bishops, successors to the other Apostles.

It is the task of the magisterium to transmit to succeeding generations divine revelation which comes to us through Sacred Scripture and Sacred Tradition, which make up a single sacred deposit of the Word of God, so that the faithful remain always faithful to the teaching of the Apostles, the brotherhood, the breaking of the bread, and the prayers. The magisterium has the additional responsibility "of giving an authentic interpretation of the Word of God, whether in its written form or in the form of Tradition, (which) has been entrusted to the living teaching office of the Church alone" (Constitution on Divine Revelation).

This authority is exercised in the name of Jesus Christ and while, like the Apostles, the magisterium acts for Jesus, this in no sense makes it the equal of Jesus or the Father, anymore than it made the Apostles equal to Jesus. If the magisterium is anything, it is a servant to the Word of God. It can teach nothing except what has been handed on to it. Those things that the magisterium proposes to the faithful for belief are drawn from the deposit of faith of which Paul spoke to Timothy.

"It is clear, therefore," sums up the Constitution on Divine Revelation, " that, in the supremely wise arrangement of God, Sacred Tradition, Sacred Scripture and the magisterium of the Church are so connected and associated that one of them cannot stand without the others. Working together, each in its own way under the action of the one Holy Spirit, they all contribute effectively to the salvation of souls."

The magisterium has the duty and obligation to speak out when controversies threaten the unity of faith and the decision it makes in matters of faith and morals is binding on all Church members. Because the pope and bishops are authentic teachers of Gospel truth, Catholics are expected to revere them as witnesses and defenders of Catholic truth and to submit to their teaching with what Vatican Council II called "respectful allegiance of mind." The faithful should be as closely attached to their bishop as the Church is to Jesus Christ, seeing in their bishop a successor of the Apostles, devoted to making known the Gospel of Jesus and that divine revelation which ceased upon the death of the last Apostle.

It can be objected that obedience to the magisterium violates the freedom of conscience. It must be pointed out that free will is God's great gift to humanity and He does not take it away even when it is abused. Theologians speak of "the authority of conscience," the manner in which the moral law is understood and acted upon. Our judgment by God depends on how our actions conform to our conscience. Therefore, God expects each person to develop an informed conscience, that is, a conscience that judges according to the truth of the will of God. We are free to believe truth or we are free to choose error, but that does not make the last choice right. There are people today who claim membership in the Flat Earth Society, who say that they believe the earth is flat. They say this despite the pictures from the spaceships which show the earth as a big blue ball spinning in space. If there is no right to do wrong (although one may choose to do it), there is no right to believe error. Jesus told us: "I am the way, and the truth, and the life; no one comes to the Father but by me" (Jn 14:6). He also told us, "If you continue in my word, you are truly my disciples, and you will know the truth, and the truth will make you free." The purpose of the magisterium and obedience is that we might know that truth in certainty, so that we can be truly free and reach the Father for all eternity. So obedience to the teaching authority of the Church is not a limitation on freedom, but its augmentation, enlarging the grasp of our intellects.

8

The Sacraments

The Catholic church is but a human organization and its "sacraments" only human invention. "For by grace are ye saved through faith" (Eph 2:8).

A sacrament is an outward sign instituted by Christ to give grace. There are seven sacraments: Baptism, Penance, Eucharist Confirmation, Marriage, Holy Orders and Anointing of the Sick —all giving grace for a particular time of life. Grace has been won for us by the merits of Jesus Christ (Jn 1:17). It is a free gift of God that bestows on us a share in God's life and is communicated to us by the Holy Spirit. Sanctifying or habitual grace comes to us primarily through the Sacraments of Initiation (Baptism, Confirmation, Eucharist). Sanctifying grace makes a person holy and pleasing to God and is necessary for salvation. The other sacraments also give sanctifying grace as well as actual sacramental grace for a particular state of life. God also gives us His grace through our prayers and good works.

Paul calls grace God's indescribable gift (1 Cor 9:15) and makes reference after reference to it throughout his letters. It is what kept him going. When he was sorely afflicted and three times begged the Lord to remove the trial from him, the Lord told him to continue bearing it because "My grace is sufficient for you." And that is what grace is for the baptized Christian. Someone once wrote as blood and air are necessary for the life of the body, God's grace is necessary for the health of the soul. It is the *sine qua non* for the spiritual life, and the follower of Jesus should do everything possible to remain in a state of grace (free of sin) and to increase in it. It is God's help to bring us to our final salvation.

St. Augustine wrote in his tract on grace (*De Natura et Gratia*): "There is no method whereby any persons arrive at absolute perfection, or whereby any man makes the slightest progress to true and godly righteousness, but by the assisting grace of our crucified Savior Christ and the gift of His Spirit; and whosoever shall deny this cannot rightly, I almost think, be reckoned in the number of any kind of Christians at all." Grace, however, does not operate in a vacuum. As St. Thomas Aquinas puts it: "A positive reality is put into a person who receives grace: there is, first, the gift freely given him, and next, his response and acknowledgment." In the same passage he adds, "Grace is a beauty of soul, which wins divine love."

Christ gave us the sacraments as means of obtaining grace, hence they become important in one's spiritual life.

Baptism

Catholics, Orthodox and most Protestants agree that Baptism is a sacrament. Baptism is the door to eternal life and to the kingdom of God. Through this sacrament the baptized is born into a new life in the Church, becomes a child of God and heir of heaven, sharing in the life of the Blessed Trinity. The baptism offered by Jesus was different from the baptism of repentance preached by John. The baptism of Jesus is a baptism of the Holy Spirit. Among the effects of Baptism is the forgiveness of original sin (the guilt passed down to us from Adam) and personal sins. It is the first of the Sacraments of Initiation, admitting the baptized into the community of the faithful.

While there is no question that Jesus established the Sacrament of Baptism, scholars differ over when this took place. Some say the sacrament was established when Jesus was baptized by John and the Holy Spirit appeared in the form of a dove above Him. Others believe it was established when Jesus told Nicodemus of the necessity of baptism, still others when Jesus began to send His disciples out on missions, and finally others in the last great command before the Ascension. In any event, the sacrament was established by Christ and made the universal sacrament of salvation when He ordered His Church: "Go therefore and make disciples of all the nations, baptizing them in the name of the Father and of the Son and of the Holy Spirit" (Mt 28:20). Each sacrament has what is called matter and form. The matter of baptism is the application of water, and the form is the words: "I baptize you in the name of the Father, and of the Son, and of the Holy Spirit." Water may be applied by immersion, pouring or sprinkling; however the current discipline of the Catholic Church only permits baptism by immersion or pouring. The ordinary minister of baptism in the Catholic Church is bishop, priest or deacon, although in the case of imminent danger of death anyone can baptize as long as the proper matter and form are used.

The Catholic Church recognizes non-Catholic baptisms that use the proper matter and form. This includes the baptism of the Orthodox churches, Old Catholics, Anglicans, Baptists, Methodists, Mennonites, Moravians, Seventh Day Adventists, among others. Mormon and Jehovah's Witnesses baptisms are not valid for lack of belief in the Christian Trinity. The Quakers, Christian Science, and Salvation Army do not baptize. Persons legitimately baptized in a non-Catholic religion are not rebaptized if they enter the Catholic Church. Baptism puts a permanent imprint on the soul of the baptized, marking that person as belonging to Christ, and thus is not repeated.

Finally, it is a very ancient custom of the Church that no one is admitted to Baptism without a godparent, described as "a member of the Christian community, who after baptism will assist the baptized to persevere in the faith and in Christian life."

Immersion

Immersion is the preferred form of Catholic baptism because as the liturgical directives say, it is "more suitable as a symbol of participation in the death and resurrection of Christ." It also symbolizes the baptized as rising from spiritual death to new life in Christ. This may have been the type of baptism used by John, and Jesus could have been baptized by immersion. Some scholars believe that Jesus merely stood in the Jordan and John poured water over His head. However, neither conclusion can be proven from the New Testament and to attempt to do so does violence to the Scriptures.

Infusion (Pouring)

Many fundamentalists make baptism by immersion almost an article of faith, but from the earliest days of the Church other methods were also used. For example, *The Teaching of the Twelve Apostles (Didache)* instructs: "Regarding baptism. Baptize as follows: after first explaining all these points, baptize in the name of the Father and of the Son and of the Holy Spirit in living water [running water]. But if you have no living water, baptize in other water, and if you cannot in cold, then in warm. But if you have neither, pour water on the head three times in the name of the Father and of the Son and of the Holy Spirit."

As mentioned earlier, the New Testament never describes the method of baptism and it must be recalled that running water is a scarce commodity in the Holy Land. There was the River Jordan in the eastern part of the holy Land and the Sea of Galilee, but outside of these bodies of water, running water was difficult to find. When Peter baptized Cornelius, the Roman centurion, and his household, the Mediterranean Sea could have been used or household water could have been supplied. Acts does not indicate the method used. In Acts 16 Paul is delivered from prison by an earthquake. The prison warden was saved from suicide by the intervention of Paul who explained the Christian faith. Despite the fact that it was after midnight, Paul baptized the jailer and his household. It is possible that there was a pool near the jail, but because of the hour of night and the darkness, it seems more probable that baptism was by infusion, although again Scripture is silent.

If Jn 3:5 is to be taken at face value, Jesus is telling Nicodemus that baptism is necessary for salvation. Unfortunately, many fundamentalists see only the words "born again," and not their qualifier. They accept only their own interpretation (immersion) of those words, and overlook the Lord's naming of baptism (water and the Spirit). Accept the validity of Jesus' statement and then people could be lost where baptism by immersion is impossible, as in certain desert areas. Many people seek baptism on their deathbed; most are so close to death that immediate baptism is mandated. Others are so sick and feeble that moving them could be fatal. Is baptism to be refused to these people because immersion is impossible? This does not seem to be the will of Jesus Christ, who wishes all people to be saved.

Infant Baptism

Infant baptism is not a scriptural doctrine, and more probably, infant baptism is more responsible for sending more people to hell than perhaps any other doctrine or religious error.

The above statement by Jimmy Swaggart in his book *Catholicism and Christianity* is a typical fundamentalist mindset. Yet I challenge any fundamentalist to submit any single Scriptural text that limits baptism to adults or denies it to children. Nevertheless, fundamentalists go beyond Scripture and limit baptism only to those who can make an adult decision to be "born again," that is, to commit his or her life to the Lord. Indeed, for the ardent fundamentalist, it is the commitment that counts, not the baptism which follows and is regarded solely as a sign of the commitment.

Fundamentalists go one step beyond. Once the commitment is made salvation is assured, a certainty many non-fundamentalists regard as a sin of presumption, believing that baptism and commitment merely open the door to salvation which also depends on what one does with the rest of his or her life. If one studies the lives of canonized saints, one sees, that despite a life of heroic sanctity, none of them ever presumed salvation but kept working towards it up to the moment of death, which came in the hope of God's mercy and justice. They remember the words of Jesus:

> *"Not everyone who says to me, 'Lord, Lord,' shall enter the kingdom of heaven, but he who does the will of my Father who is in heaven. On the last day many will say to me, 'Lord, Lord, did not we prophesy in your name, and cast out demons in your name, and do many mighty works in your name?' And then I will declare to them, 'I never knew you; depart from me you evildoers.'" (Mt 7:21-23)*

No, salvation depends on more than being "born again." It is the constant doing of the will of the Father and it is in this daily obedience that sanctity is realized.

The necessity of infant baptism is demonstrated by its effects:

1. *Incorporation into new life* (Rom 6:4-5). Baptism prints an indelible mark on the soul that stamps the bearer as belonging to Jesus Christ. Even though the person may later sin or even apostatize, this imprint of possession remains. Cannot a child belong to Jesus?

2. *Forgiveness of original and personal sin.* No one in the state of sin can enter heaven. It was to redeem us from the sin of Adam and from our own personal sins that Jesus came upon earth. Is this redemption to be denied a child? Eternal salvation could be at stake.

3. *Incorporation into the Church.* Faith is expressed through the community of believers which is a means of growth in faith and holiness. This process of growth begins at birth. Peter (1 Pt 2:1-5) tells us we must grow into salvation. Yet there are those who would postpone this for children.

4. *The bestowal of sacramental grace.* Grace is necessary for the life and development of the soul. The grace that comes through baptism belongs to all. No one interested in the welfare of a child would deny it the physical nourishment needed for growth, yet "adult only" baptism does this to the child's spiritual development.

While only-adult baptism cannot be justified by Scripture, the word of God does give a strong inference of infant baptism. In Acts 16:33 Paul baptizes his jailer and the man's family in the small hours of the morning. The baptism of Cornelius, the centurion, by Peter (Acts 10:48) is a multiple baptism. Later in Acts (18:8) Paul baptizes Crispus, a synagogue official, along with his household. In 1 Cor 1:16 Paul mentions that he baptized "the household of Stephanus." Evidently baptizing entire families was a common practice and it is difficult to imagine that none of these families had children. In another place (Sol 2:11-12) Paul likens baptism to Jewish circumcision and the Jews did circumcise infants, so it is quite reasonable to deduce that this practice was carried over into Christian baptism.

Non-Water Forms of Baptism

In 1 Tim 2:4-6 Paul writes that God wills everyone to be saved. This raises the question of what happens to people who do not know God's will in this regard. The Catholic Church teaches that these people can be saved by baptism of desire. A person who lives according to the will of God, as he or she understands it, who desires to do what God wants and hence would be baptized if the person knew this to be God's will, attains salvation on the basis of this baptism of desire. This is in effect a baptism of conscience which the Church has always held as inviolate.

The other method of baptism is baptism of blood. This arose in the earliest Church when Christians and catechumens (people preparing for baptism) gave their lives rather than deny Jesus Christ. Many of these catechumens were slain before they could be baptized. Since that time it has been a constant Tradition of the Church that those who give their lives for Jesus are baptized in blood.

Confirmation

In the Sacrament of Confirmation initiation into the life of Jesus and the Church is completed. Confirmation is a sacrament wherein the Holy Spirit is given to the baptized by the imposition of hands, the anointing with chrism, while saying the words, "Be sealed with the gift of the Holy Spirit." A bishop is the ordinary minister of this sacrament. The matter of the sacrament is the anointing with chrism in the sign of the cross on the forehead and the form is the above words. In this sacrament baptismal promises are renewed and the person confirmed is directed to take his or her responsible role in the Church by living the teachings of Jesus Christ. It is a point in the spiritual development of the Christian when an informed decision is made to live fully the Christian life. The sacrament corresponds in some ways to the Jewish bar mitzvah or the fundamentalist being "born again."

The very essence of this sacrament is the reception of the

Holy Spirit, who played so intimate a role in the mission of Jesus (Mk 1:10 and Jn 1:32). Jesus promised His disciples that the Holy Spirit would strengthen them (Lk 12:12) and would remain with them forever (Jn 14:16). Jesus renewed His promise of the Holy Spirit immediately before His Ascension (Acts 1:8). This promise was fulfilled on Pentecost when the Apostles were transformed from frightened men into witnesses for Christ and went forth to proclaim "the mighty works of God."

In the early Church this sacrament was called "laying on of hands" (Heb 6:2) and was the prerogative of the Apostles (bishops). The Book of Acts (8:4 ff) tells us that the apostolate of the deacon Philip in Samaria was so successful that the Apostles Peter and John went to Samaria where they prayed over the new converts that they might receive the Holy Spirit, "Then they laid hands on them and they received the Holy Spirit." The Catholic Church repeats this action today in the Sacrament of Confirmation.

While the Western Church delays confirmation for informed consent, the Eastern Church includes it with Baptism. Although the surrounding rites have changed over the centuries, the essence of the sacrament is apostolic. This giving of the Holy Spirit confirms believers more perfectly to Christ and strengthens them so that they may bear witness to Christ. In receiving this sacrament they are so marked with the character or seal of the Lord that the Sacrament of Confirmation, like Baptism, cannot be repeated.

Marriage

The family is the basic unit of society. In the family husband and wife share in God's creative power and share in the spiritual love which God wills. It is unfortunate that today's pagan world has distorted the word "love," which is another word for God, into a synonym for a sexual act that may be far removed from

70

true spiritual love. Hence, the Church's view of marriage as a sacrament is ever more important today.

Theologians disagree as to the exact time Jesus established this sacrament. Some incline to the view that He raised the marriage contract to a sacrament when He sanctified by His presence the wedding in Cana (Jn 2:2). Others believe it was when He nullified the bill of separation permitted by Moses (Mk 10). Others hold it was in the oral Tradition passed by the Apostles, given them by Christ after His resurrection. Paul (Eph 5:23) likens marriage to the union of Christ and His Church. He speaks frequently of Christian marriage and in 1 Cor 7 gives lengthy advice to the married.

Marriage is a sacrament which is not ministered by a priest but by the couple being married. The remote matter of Christian marriage is a baptized bride and groom, free to marry. The proximate matter is the marriage contract. The form is the acceptance of each ("I do") of the marriage contract. Any other marriage does not have sacramental character and is a natural contract only, The essential properties of marriage are unity and indissolubility.

Many Christians today do not recognize the indissolubility of marriage; this includes some fundamentalists. However, the Catholic Church must be true to the teaching of Christ, who said marriage can only be dissolved by death. In a discussion of marriage He told the Pharisees (Mk 10:9): "What therefore God has joined together, let not man put asunder." In the next verse He instructs His Apostles: "Whoever divorces his wife and marries another, commits adultery against her; and if she divorces her husband and marries another, she commits adultery."

Because of this teaching the Catholic Church does not recognize divorce and forbids its members to divorce and remarry. In certain cases a legal separation is allowed but never remarriage. This has caused some to leave the Church, the most notable being Henry VIII, who was refused a divorce by the pope. An annulment to an existing marriage, that is, a finding after examination by an ecclesiastical court, with a canon lawyer defending the bond, that there was never a marriage in the first place, can be given by the court, and if it is upheld in a second court, the parties involved are declared never married. In such a case it must be proven that there was a preexisting cause that invalidated the marriage and prevented it from taking place. Such an invalidating cause could be failure to consummate the marriage, entering marriage through force (duress) or grave fear, impotency, an already existing bond, concealed disparity of worship, attempted marriage by a priest or deacon, consanguinity, etc. There is a whole body of canon law dealing with this matter.

In order to avoid an invalid marriage and to properly prepare a couple to enter Christian marriage, canon law requires a pastoral preparation for marriage to be given by the pastors, so that maturity and true Christian commitment is possessed by those entering marriage. Many parishes now have marriage preparation courses to insure assistance and education for those preparing to marry, utilizing the experience of married couples, doctors, psychologists, and others skilled in marriage problems and counseling. The Church believes such preparation is necessary in view of the social, economic, and civil climate today which promotes a lifestyle rooted in money, hedonism, action, and power.

Holy Orders

There is absolutely no mention of priests in the New Testament church. Jesus made the position of the earthly priest obsolete.

Holy Orders is a sacrament of the New Law whereby the imposition of hands on a baptized male person confers spiritual powers and the grace to use them worthily. The matter of the sacrament is the imposition of hands and the form the actual words of ordination. The minister of Holy Orders is a validly ordained bishop. Holy Orders refers to the ordination of bishop, priest, and deacon.

By His own free election Jesus chose the Twelve to be His assistants and share in His mission in a particular way (Mk 3:14).

After His resurrection Jesus reconfirmed this special calling to preach, baptize, and forgive sin (Mt 28:19-20, Mk 16:15-16, Jn 20:22-23). Jesus also gave His Apostles the right to expand the Church and ordain helpers and successors. Thus in the very first chapter of Acts the eleven surviving Apostles pick a successor to Judas Iscariot. When another type of successor was needed, the Apostles accepted seven candidates for the new order of deacon, and as Acts 6:6 tells us, the Apostles "prayed and laid hands on them." Later in Chapter 13:3 Paul and Barnabas are ordained. In 2 Tim 1:6 Paul bids Timothy "rekindle the gift of God that is within you through the laying on of my hands." 1 Tim 4:14 tells us that other elders were with Paul when this ordination took place.

To claim that there were no priests in the Apostolic Church is simply an ignorance of language. The Greek word *presbyter* which is used in the New Testament means priest or, as some translate it, elder. The house in which priests live is called a presbytery. In 1 Tim Paul gives qualifications for bishop and deacon. In Chapter 5:17-22 he gives rules for priests. In Titus 1 Paul tells Bishop Titus to appoint priests in every town "as I directed you."

Webster's New Collegiate Dictionary defines presbyter as a member of the order of priests in churches having episcopal hierarchies, including bishops, priests and deacons. To deny that priests existed in the New Testament is simply an ignorance of New Testament language.

Anointing of the Sick

Jesus designed His sacraments to meet various needs one passes through in life. Baptism at birth, Confirmation in youth, Matrimony or Holy Orders for adulthood, and Anointing of the Sick when the danger of death approaches.

The Gospels are full of Jesus' compassion for the sick and the miracles He worked on their behalf. When He sent His Apostles and disciples on missions, He gave them instruction to cure the sick (Mt 10:8). "And they cast out many demons, and anointed with oil many that were sick and healed them" (Mk 6:13). Examples of the Apostles caring for the sick are given in the Book of Acts. St. James in his letter instructs Christians (Jas 5:14-15): "Is any among you sick? Let him call for the elders [presbyters] of the church, and let them pray over him, anointing him with oil in the name of the Lord; and the prayers of faith will save the sick man, and the Lord will raise him up; and if he has committed sins, he will be forgiven."

What James describes is the Sacrament of the Anointing of the Sick as practiced by the Catholic Church and in which sins are forgiven and bodily health prayed for. The recipients of this sacrament are Christians suffering serious illness, and persons with infirmities due to old age. The sacrament can be repeated if a person is again in serious danger from the same illness. After a silent imposition of hands the priest anoints with consecrated oil the forehead and hands of the sick person, saying: "Through this holy anointing may the Lord in His love and mercy help you with the grace of the Holy Spirit. Amen. May the Lord who frees you from sin save you and raise you up. Amen." The matter of the sacrament is the anointing with oil and the form the words said.

9

Confession

God has never given any person the authority to make a decision as to whether to forgive or retain another person's sins. "For there is one God, and one mediator between God and man, the man Christ Jesus" (1 Tim 2:5).

First of all, the above Scripture, although incomplete, is one with which all Catholics would agree. It is the heart of Paul's theology that Jesus Christ is the Father's chosen mediator, the center of God's plan of salvation; the perfect Redeemer who satisfied for our sins. It is Jesus who restored an alienated humanity to life and peace with the Father. But the fact that Jesus is the one Mediator does not deny Him from choosing others to assist Him in this work. He selected the Twelve to assist Him, and as Acts tells us, the Apostles continued the work of the Master and in turn chose successors to continue it through time. Thus others do assist Jesus in this mediation but only in secondary roles and, as *The Teaching of Christ* says, "in total dependence on Jesus, for He is the necessary and indispensable mediator." Sins are forgiven us because of the sacrifice of and redemption by Jesus. No one can forgive sins in his own name, but only in the name of Jesus. It is as representatives of Jesus that Catholic priests have the power to forgive sins, a power given to His Apostles and through the Apostles to duly ordained priests.

Fundamentalists have a great deal of trouble with confession, or what Catholics call Reconciliation or the Sacrament of

Penance. They quote the above verse from Timothy and when backed down on that reply that anyway auricular confession did not exist until the Lateran Council mandated it in 1215. They overlook the fact that oral confession existed in the early Church and what the Lateran Council mandated was not confession but annual confession for all Catholics. Origen, writing about A.D. 240 in his homily on Leviticus, praised the Catholic "who does not shrink from confessing his sin to a priest of the Lord." About the same time St. Cyprian, writing on faults, advised Christians to "confess to the priests of God in an honest way and in sorrow, making an open disclosure of conscience." So it is wrong to assert that oral confession did not exist until medieval times or was started by Irish monks, or to give any of the other reasons to justify an existing bias.

Some of the arguments put forth about confession become a bit absurd. Jimmy Swaggart asks, for example, "Did the Apostle Peter give absolution to Cornelius (Acts 10)? Did the Apostle Paul give absolution to the Philippian jailer (Acts 16)?" His answer is of course, "No." A correct answer, but for the wrong reason. Either his reply is deceitful or he doesn't understand the nature of Baptism. Both Cornelius and the jailer were being baptized, and confession is not necessary for baptism since Baptism in itself forgives sin.

The fundamentalist will rebut Catholic statements about confession by saying, "I can confess my sins directly to God." Of course, he can. And his sins will be forgiven provided he has true repentance for his alienation from God, coupled with a firm resolution to avoid these sins in the future. But can he be sure he had the proper disposition for the forgiveness of sin? Can he have absolute certainty the sins were forgiven? If the word of Christ is to believed, this certainty can come in the Sacrament of Penance.

Catholic certainty about the power of priests to forgive sin is rooted in the grant from Christ, given on the night of the resurrection when he appeared to the Twelve, breathed on them and said:

> "*Receive the Holy Spirit. If you forgive the sins of any, they are forgiven. If you retain the sins of any, they are retained*" (*Jn 20:22-23*).

Now one either accepts these words of Christ at face value or one rejects them. Some object, like Swaggart, that the translation is bad, that the Greek does not say what the English says. These objectors are in effect accusing the scholars who have translated the Scriptures as incompetents when they themselves have no credentials of proficiency in Greek or Aramaic. What John is describing here, using the Greek *pneuma* (breath, spirit) is the intimate connection between the resurrection and the animation of the Church that will inherit His mission. This Spirit will enable the Church to carry on the judicial character of Christ (Jn 5:27) in the matter of sin (Mt. 9:6, etc.). This power is different from the power given previously to Peter of binding and loosing, which is broad power in matters of faith and morals. The power transferred on Easter night is limited to sin. The breathing on the Apostles shows the sacramental intention of Jesus.

Jesus gave His rallying cry at the beginning of His mission: "Repent, and believe in the Gospel" (Mk 1:15). Repentance is the beginning of conversion and conversion is an ongoing process, just as belief is the beginning of action which goes beyond one's deed. Conversion is more than merely being "born again," and belief is empty without deeds. Even despite good intentions, we can fail Christ, and we must be careful not to deceive ourselves. As 1 John 1:8-10 tells us about confessions: "If we say we have no sin, we deceive ourselves, and the truth is not in us. If we confess our sins, he is faithful and just, and will cleanse us from all unrighteousness. If we say we have not sinned, we make him a liar, and his word is not in us."

The Church's Confession of Faith puts it this way: "We often experience in painful ways that we fall short in our following of Jesus Christ, that we even place ourselves in contradiction to what we Christians should be and do according to God's will. Instead of letting ourselves be led by the Spirit of Christ, we often follow the 'spirit of the world.' Yet God's mercy is greater than all sin and guilt. He offers even those who have fallen into serious sin after baptism *another possibility for a change of life and for grace."* This is the Sacrament of Penance. The Church Fathers often speak of it as "a second, toilsome baptism, a second plank of salvation after the shipwreck of sin."

The mission of Jesus was the reconciliation of God and humanity, fractured by the disobedience of Adam and the continued waywardness of mankind. This act of reconciliation is ongoing because the sin of humans is ongoing. In Christ's Sacrament of Penance the faithful "obtain from the mercy of God pardon for their sins against Him; at the same time they are reconciled with the Church which they wounded by their sins and which works for their conversion by charity, example, and prayer" (*Lumen Gentium* 11). Through Penance the sinner redirects his life to the Father "who first loved us" (1 John 4:19), to Christ who died for us, and to the Holy Spirit whose graces we have received in abundance (Titus 2:6). Penance, therefore, continues the act of conversion and renews in the sinner the intention to lead a new life. This intention is made known to the Church through the words of the sacrament, which to be effective must have certain form.

1. *Contrition.* The most important disposition of the penitent is contrition — heartfelt sorrow and aversion for the sin —accompanied by the resolve of avoiding the sin in the future. There can be no forgiveness of sin unless we have sorrow for sin and resolve to undergo a change of life, a repentance the Greek calls *metanoia.* This sorrow must be an interior sorrow, not merely

verbal expression (Mt 7:21). The sorrow arises from a motive of faith. Contrition is called "perfect" when it arises from love of God and regrets the offense given God. It is called "imperfect" when it arises out of a lesser motive, such as regret for punishment brought about by sin.

2. *Confession.* Having prepared himself or herself, the penitent confesses those sins which alienate from God and the Church. In opening one's heart to the minister of God, spiritual judgment can be made in accordance with the power of the keys. Excessive detail is neither required nor recommended; merely enough so the confessor can judge the gravity of the offense.

3. *Act of Penance.* Conversion is shown by making satisfaction for one's failure and reparation for an injury, suited to one's personal condition. "Therefore, it is necessary that the act of penance really be a remedy for sin and a help to renewal of life. Thus the penitent, 'forgetting the things that are behind him' (Philippians 3:13), again becomes part of the mystery of salvation and turns himself towards the future" (*Decree on Penance*).

4. *Absolution.* Through the words of absolution and the Sign of the Cross made over the penitent by the priest, God grants pardon to the sinner and the Sacrament of Penance is completed. In this sacrament God welcomes home the prodigal child who has strayed from Him, Christ places the lost sheep on His shoulders and returns it to the sheepfold, and there is joy in the Church over one who has returned from afar. The absolution is the form of the sacrament.

There are many kinds of personal sins: sins of commission or omission; sins in thought, word, or deed; sins of ignorance and weakness; sins of malice; sins against the Holy Spirit: despair, presumption, resisting known truth, obstinacy, impenitence; sins crying to heaven for vengeance: murder, sodomy, defrauding workers of a just wage, oppression of widows and orphans; capital or root sins (from which other sins come): pride, envy, anger, covetousness, lust, gluttony, sloth. There are social sins and sins against faith. There are internal sins (those committed in the mind, having the same gravity as actually committed sin [Mt 5:28]) and external sins (committed in act). It would take page upon page to try and categorize them all.

Sin is judged according to its gravity as either mortal or venial. A mortal (deadly) sin is one which cuts the sinner off from life with God. Mortal sin involves grave (serious) matter, full advertence (knowing the matter is grave and deliberately choosing it over friendship with God), and full consent of the will.

This type of sin is called mortal because if one dies in mortal sin, one dies rejecting God and hence will be separated from Him for all eternity. A venial sin is a less serious offense which lessens the fervor of charity. It is not a rejection of God, nor does it concern a serious matter. All mortal sins must be confessed, and, while confession of venial sins is not required, it is recommended that a penitent do so, in order that the confessor can give advice to avoid their repetition. Venial sins can be forgiven outside confession by an act of contrition to God (telling God you are sorry and intend to do better) or in a penance service, such as one that begins the eucharistic liturgy.

It is Church law to confess at least once a year, but this only applies when mortal sin is present. However, more frequent confession (at least once a month) is recommended, even though mortal sin is absent. The reasons are severalfold. For one, the sacrament, like all sacraments, gives grace which makes us sensitive to God's law and aids us as we try to live His commands in our daily lives. A second reason is that confession keeps our consciences sensitive. By examining my conscience before confession, as I am expected to do, I keep my conscience alert to faults.

Conscience can become numb and insensitive by continual repetition of some act displeasing to God. Confession gives one the opportunity to resensitize conscience. Finally, each confession is a point in time when we can begin anew, freed from the past, in our love for Jesus. Frequent confession is a remarkable help in the growth of one's spiritual life, and we should use the assistance Jesus willed to give us.

10

The Eucharist

Catholics think the host and wine actually become His [Jesus'] personal flesh and blood, so they worship bread — a form of idolatry. The celebration of the Eucharist is labeled a "sacrifice," due partly to the pagan custom of calling everything offered to gods a sacrifice. Christ died once and for all time but Catholics seek to perpetuate that death.

Fundamentalists rightly center their dislike of things Catholic on the doctrine of the Eucharist, and this is rightly so because the Eucharist is at the core of Catholic practice. This disdain is confusing to Catholics who have some knowledge of fundamentalism and its regard for Scripture — confusing because to them the Eucharist is one of the most scriptural and logical teachings of Jesus.

Jesus was a masterful teacher, who understood the working of the human psyche. He brought attention to His teaching by miracles and revelations, by parables and visual aids. When He was ready to proclaim His doctrine of the Eucharist (from a Greek word meaning to show favor), He prepared well for it. First, He worked the miracle of feeding four thousand (Mk 8). Then in John 6 He works a second feeding miracle for five thousand, an immediate preparation for what He will announce the following day.

The next day (Jn 6), after the miracle of the five thousand, the crowd has sought out Jesus again. He tells them that they were seeking Him not because they understood His signs of preparation but because they had their fill to eat, adding they should be concerned not with food that perishes but with that food which endures for eternal life. The Jews, thinking of the manna God gave their ancestors in the desert, want Jesus to work a similar miracle for them.

"My Father gives you the true bread from heaven," Jesus replies. "For the bread of God is that which comes down from heaven and gives life to the world."

They say to Him, "Lord, give us this bread always."

Then Jesus declares, "I am the bread of life. I am the living bread which came down from heaven; if any one eats of this bread, he will live forever; and the bread that I shall give for the life of the world is my flesh."

This statement shocked the Jews, and they began arguing among themselves, "How can this man give us his flesh to eat?" The Jews accepted the words of Christ literally; they did not think He was speaking symbolically or figuratively.

Jesus did not correct their interpretation, knowing that they had understood Him. "Truly, truly," He replied, ". . . unless you eat the flesh of the Son of man and drink His blood, you have no life in you; he who eats my flesh and drinks my blood . . . abides in me and I in him. He who eats this bread will live forever."

The teaching scandalized the Jews, and the crowd dispersed. With them went some of the disciples of Jesus who could not accept the literalness of His statements. Jesus did not call them back and say, "Look, I was only talking in symbols; don't take me literally." No, He let them go.

Then He turned to the Twelve and asked, "Will you also go away?"

"Lord, to whom shall we go?" replied Peter, spokesman for the group. "You have the words of eternal life; and we have believed, and have come to know, that you are the Holy One of God."

In His sermon Jesus spoke of "the bread that I shall give,"

meaning that the bestowal of this bread was in the future. That future arrived at the Last Supper. Mark describes it this way:

> *And as they were eating, he took bread, and blessed and broke it, and gave it to them and said, "Take; this is my body." And he took a cup, and when he had given thanks he gave it to them, and they all drank of it. And he said to them, "This is my blood of the covenant, which is poured out for many."*

Luke (Lk 22:19-20) gives this account:

> *And he took bread, and when he had given thanks he broke it and gave it to them, saying, "This is my body which is given for you. Do this in remembrance of me." And likewise the cup after supper, saying, "This cup which is poured out for you is the new covenant in my blood."*

Christ's "Do this" clearly shows He was instituting a rite that He wanted to carry on. The apostolic Church understood this and called the ceremony the Breaking of the Bread and the Lord's Supper. The Fathers referred to it as the Eucharist. The word "Mass" is of later origin, coming from the dismissal, "*Ite, missa est* (Go, it is sent)." The word *missa* is from the Latin *mittere*, to send. In the dismissal, with the prayer already sent, Christians were sent forth to live the teachings of Christ and spread His Gospel.

Paul gives a clear description of what this ceremony meant in the early Church when he writes in 1 Cor 11:23-27:

> *For I received from the Lord what I also delivered to you, that the Lord Jesus on the night when he was betrayed took bread, and when he had given thanks, he broke it, and said: "This is my body which is for you. Do this in*

remembrance of me." In the same way also the cup, after supper, saying, "This cup is the new covenant in my blood. Do this, as often as you drink it, in remembrance of me." For as often as you eat this bread and drink this cup, you proclaim the Lord's death until he comes. Whoever, therefore, eats the bread or drinks the cup is an unworthy manner will be guilty of profaning the body and blood of the Lord.

These texts, joined and simplified, make up the Consecration of the Catholic Mass. Other ceremonies have developed over the centuries surrounding this act, but it is the Consecration which is the essence of the Mass and gives it validity. The Mass text is this (with the essential words capitalized):

The day before he suffered
(The priest takes the bread and raising it a little above the altar, continues:)
he took bread in his sacred hands and looking up to heaven, to you, his almighty Father, he gave you thanks and praise. He broke the bread, gave it to his disciples, and said:
TAKE THIS, ALL OF YOU, AND EAT IT: THIS IS MY BODY WHICH WILL BE GIVEN UP FOR YOU.
(Then he continues:)
When supper was ended,
(He takes the chalice and, raising it a little above the altar, continues:)
he took the cup. Again he gave you thanks and praise, gave the cup to his disciples, and said:
TAKE THIS, ALL OF YOU, AND DRINK FROM IT: THIS IS THE CUP OF MY BLOOD, THE BLOOD OF THE NEW AND EVERLASTING COVENANT. IT WILL BE SHED FOR YOU AND FOR ALL SO THAT

SINS MAY BE FORGIVEN. DO THIS IN MEMORY OF ME.

These texts when taken together show the progressive doctrine of the Eucharist as revealed by Jesus. Over the centuries people have tried to explain away this teaching because they do not come to it with an open mind. They play semantic games which have no foundation in fact. They take other Scripture texts out of context or distort their sense, seemingly not aware that Scripture does not contradict itself. Perhaps for many the problem lies in the fact that the Eucharist, like the Trinity and the Incarnation, is a mystery and therefore not fully understandable, and that it must be accepted on faith in the word of Jesus. A theological mystery (Greek, *mysterion*, something closed) is a hidden or secret thing of a sacred character. The divine mysteries by their very nature so surpass the created intellect that, even when revealed and believed, they remain obscure and veiled in this life. Thus a mystery can only be known by revelation while its essence cannot be fully understood or explained after revelation. God is infinite and omniscient, and the finite mind cannot comprehend infinite truth. So we accept the fact of a mystery in faith, a faith in this case rooted in the word of the Son of God. Thus in the Mass, immediately after the Consecration the priest says or sings: "Let us proclaim the mystery of faith." The people then respond with their belief.

The enemies of the Mass accuse it of being a pagan rite (when in reality the whole Mass is a very scriptural action); say that Catholics believe they kill Christ over and over (Christ was appointed only once to die, and the Mass is a memorial of His death, which Paul tells us to proclaim over and over); bring charges of cannibalism against Catholics (the body of Jesus ascended to heaven — what Catholics receive under the appearance of bread and wine — is the mystery of the Eucharist).

Regarding the last charge (one, incidentally, that goes back to pagan Rome and shows Christian belief in the reality of the sacrament), again the reality is veiled in mystery that we accept on the word of Jesus.

Fundamentalists should examine the Last Supper. Jesus was present there in His physical body, yet He spoke of the bread He was holding as His body and the wine as His blood — Jesus in two places at the same time. Fundamentalists don't understand it, and I can't explain it, but that is the nature of mystery. I believe in Jesus and I believe in His word, and that is what faith is. Yet faith itself is a gift of God and one must be properly disposed to receive it, and this requires an open mind. Vatican Council II observed so wisely: "Before people can come to the liturgy they must be called to faith and conversion. 'But how are men to call upon him in whom they have not believed?' (Rom 10:14)."

The introduction to the instruction on the Eucharist (*Eucharisticum mysterium*) issued by the Congregation for Divine Worship of the Holy See summarizes Catholic Doctrine on the Eucharist:

"The celebration of the Eucharist is the center of the entire Christian life, both for the Church universal and for the local congregations of the Church. 'The other sacraments, all the ministries of the Church, and the works of the apostolate are united with the Eucharist and directed toward it. For the holy Eucharist contains the entire spiritual treasure of the Church, that is, Christ himself, our passover and living bread.' "

11

Purgatory

What does the word of God say concerning purgatory? Nothing. The Roman Catholic doctrine of purgatory is purely pagan and cannot stand in the light of Scripture.

Purgatory is one of the most vehement arguments used against the Church by fundamentalists, particularly in attempts to convert Catholics. The argument is rooted in the fact that the word purgatory is never mentioned in the Bible, although exactly what that proves, particularly if such a place is described, is not clear. You will not find the word "Trinity" mentioned in the Bible, but the Trinity is a fundamental Christian doctrine, as is the Incarnation, another word unknown from Scripture. Fundamentalists believe in heaven and hell as do Catholics, but the Church goes a step beyond and says there is also an intermediate place of atonement and purification called purgatory.

God forgives, but God does not forget. What God knows, He knows for all eternity. God forgives our sins through our repentance, but at the same time He demands reparation for these offenses. Hence, we have to distinguish between forgiveness and atonement. It is like a boy who hits a ball through his parents' window while playing baseball. He tells his mother that he is sorry. She replies, "I know you didn't do it on purpose, so you are forgiven. However, you were careless and I expect you to pay for a new window out of your allowance." She does this because it is just and she wishes to teach her son responsibility for his acts. Reparation for sin is one way God teaches us responsibility. When God is offended by our acts, His mercy will bring us forgiveness but His justice demands atonement, which, if not done in this life, must be done in the next before entering heaven. This place of atonement is called purgatory, the place where one is purged or cleansed from the remnants of sin.

Revelation (21:27) tells us nothing unclean shall enter heaven. Jesus reveals that only the pure of heart shall see God (Mt 5:8). Yet few of us die perfect, and perfection is necessary to be in the presence of All-Perfection. Most of us die with some attachment to sin. We die with our pride, our failures in charity, our lack of prayerfulness, our human weaknesses. These are small defects, not willed as an alienation from God, or cause for us to be sent to an eternity in hell, but defects nonetheless which must be removed if we are to enter the abode of the saints (those without imperfections). The place where the removal of these defects takes place we call purgatory.

Graffiti, made by early Christians in the catacómbs of Rome, ask Christians passing by to pray for deceased relatives. But there is no point in praying for those in heaven, who have all the beatitude they can contain, nor is there any point in praying for those consigned to all eternity in hell, from which there is no return. These early Christians believed that souls of the departed were in an intermediate place awaiting entrance into heaven — purgatory.

In 2 Mac 12:46 we read that a collection taken up by Judas Maccabeus to obtain prayers for the dead was "a holy and pious thought" and that through it "he made atonement for the dead, that they might be delivered from their sin." As stated earlier, Catholics accept Maccabees as the inspired word of God, but Protestants do not. Nevertheless, it shows Jewish thought in the century before the Christian era and proves that while Catholics may have coined the word purgatory, they did not invent the idea.

Catholics see a number of allusions to purgatory in Scripture.

For example, in Mt 12:32 Jesus speaks of a sin that "will not be forgiven, either in this age or the age to come." The inference here is that there are some sins that will be forgiven after death — sins not properly repented nor atoned for but not serious enough to cause everlasting death, yet which can be purified by suffering separation from God.

While the Church has defined the existence of purgatory, it has not defined its nature, and this is an open theological question. Some of the early teachers — St. Gregory of Nyssa, St. Gregory the Great, St. Augustine, among others — speak of the cleansing fire of purgatory. Others — St. Catherine of Genoa, St. Bonaventure, for example — saw the suffering of purgatory as spiritual pain — separation from God but not without hope. As St. Catherine puts it, "The soul in purgatory feels great happiness and great sorrow; the one does not hinder the other." The happiness is caused by the knowledge that salvation is attained, the sadness because one is not yet in the presence of God. Most Western theologians today reject the notion of real fire, as does the Eastern Church, but the exact nature of the suffering is still debated.

The Church's Confession of Faith speaks of the pain of purgatory this way: "The talk of purgatorial fire is an image that refers to a deeper reality. Fire can be understood as the cleansing, purifying, and sanctifying power of God's holiness and mercy. The encounter with the fire of God's love that takes place in death has a purifying and transforming power for the man who has indeed decided for God in principle but who has not consistently realized this decision and has fallen short of the ideal. Is this not the case for almost everyone? God's power straightens, purifies, heals, and consummates whatever remained imperfect at death. Purgatory is God himself as purifying and sanctifying power for man."

How long is the soul in purgatory? The Church is silent on the issue. The psalmist tells us that in the sight of God a thousand years are but a day. For the soul cut off from full life with God a day could seem like a thousand years. This is matter left to God's mercy and justice.

The fundamentalist's distaste for purgatory is based primarily on his "only Scripture" beliefs and an inherited Protestant disesteem for this doctrine that traces back to the Reformation, when the reformers connected it with abuses in the matter of indulgences and were so incensed against this abuse that they were led to throw the baby out with the bathwater. Martin Luther was not opposed to purgatory, although he did at one point call it "an uncertainty." However, John Calvin railed against the notion and saw it as "a dreadful blasphemy against Christ." His objection was based in the fact that the sufferings of Jesus Christ were sufficient for the forgiveness of all sin. But, as was pointed out above, there is a difference between forgiveness and reparation, and this distinction escaped Calvin. Paul seems to approach this distinction in 1 Cor 3:11-15 when he speaks of Jesus as the unique foundation of the Church and says that those who succeed him must build on that foundation. The preacher who fails this test will suffer a loss but can be saved. The "fire" of the passage suggests an expiatory punishment for faults not meriting damnation.

The Church divides its membership into three groups: the Church triumphant (the saints in heaven), the Church militant (the faithful on earth still struggling against self and the temptations of Satan), and the Church suffering (those in purgatory), all forming the Mystical Body of Christ (1 Cor 12:27). As Paul tells us, "If one member suffers, all suffer together; if one member is honored, all rejoice together" (1 Cor 12;26). The mystical identification of Christ with the members of the Church and the identification of the members with one another make it possible for members in the Church militant to offer prayer and sacrifices for members in need, both living and in purgatory. Just as Paul added his sufferings (Col 1:24) to the sufferings of Christ for the sake of the Church, so we too can add our sufferings and prayers for the good of its members. Catholics do this in various ways.

While there have been past (and perhaps some present) abuses rising from the doctrine on purgatory, these should not blind one to the validity of the doctrine itself. The Council of Trent ruled that bishops should only allow sound doctrine on purgatory to be taught and they should "prohibit as scandals and stumbling blocks to the faithful those matters which tend to certain curiosity or superstition, or that savor of filthy lucre." Hence, bishops are always on watch for abuses. The frequent accusation that the Catholic Church supports itself on the doctrine of purgatory does not stand up under an examination of the facts, but it is bruited abroad with such vehemence and frequency that many accept the charge as fact.

Catholics base the doctrine of purgatory largely on Tradition, the authenticity of which was discussed earlier. Even though fundamentalists do not accept Tradition, they can through the application of logic come to accept the notion of a place of final preparation for entering heaven. As in Sirach's advice (7:33), let them "Give graciously to all the living and withhold not kindness from the dead."

Closely associated with the teaching on purgatory is the Church's practice of granting indulgences to the faithful, which the person gaining the indulgence can apply to the dead. These grants lead to more misunderstandings than even purgatory itself does.

Indulgences

> An indulgence is a permit to commit sin, given by the Roman church to its members.

To offset the above notion, which is not infrequently heard, let me at the outset define what an indulgence is so that the reader will know what is being talked about. An indulgence is the partial or total remission before God of temporal punishment due to already forgiven sins, which the Catholic can gain by the performance of a meritorious act to which the indulgence is attached. To gain an indulgence one must be free of serious unforgiven sin, and in the matter of a full indulgence, besides the meritorious act, confession, Holy Communion and prayer for the intention of the pope are required. Hence, Catholic understanding of an indulgence is the exact opposite of the accusation that begins this section.

It was the matter of indulgences that was the immediate cause of the Protestant Reformation. The Dominican friar John Tetzel entered the Germanic states bearing a letter from Pope Leo X, issued in 1516, which granted an indulgence for the dead to those who contributed towards the completion of St. Peter's Basilica in Rome. This greatly disturbed Martin Luther, who denounced Tetzel's crusade and the impression he gave that all one had to do to gain the indulgence was to make a donation of money. Tetzel never mentioned confession and the renunciation of sin as a condition, so Luther's objection had validity. The German priest was so incensed that it led him to post his ninety-five theses on the door of a Wittenberg church, and the Protestant revolt was underway. Although Tetzel's offense was prohibited by general laws on simony, there was no specific law regarding indulgences. The Council of Trent (1562) rectified that lapse, and since then the buying or selling of indulgences has been forbidden. The same council, reacting to the Protestant attack, did decree "that the use of indulgences, most salutary for Christian people and approved by the authority of sacred councils, is to be retained in the Church; and it condemns with anathema those who either assert they are useless or deny that there is in the Church power for granting them."

As discussed above concerning purgatory, every sin brings punishment that must be atoned for in this life or the next. This is the reason that penances are given to people as part of confession. The penance is a form of atonement assigned by the confessor. However, one does not know if the atonement made is completely satisfactory or even if it was done with fully proper disposition. If not, the atonement must be completed in purgatory. As St. Augustine (354-430) wrote, "Every sin, whether great or small, must be punished either by man himself doing penance or by God chastising him."

Indulgences for the dead flow from the doctrine of Communion of Saints, which is "the mutual sharing of help, expiation, prayers, and benefits among the faithful who, whether they are already in possession of their heavenly fatherland or are detained in purgatory or are still living as pilgrims on earth, are united and form one commonwealth, whose head is Christ, whose form is charity" (Pope Leo XIII 1902). This ability to touch one another seems something the Christian knows instinctively: a mother prays for her children; children pray for their parents.

The doctrine of the Communion of Saints leads to another teaching: the Treasury of the Church. This treasury is not a material one but refers to the merits and graces earned by Jesus and the saints, "offered so that all of mankind could be set free from sin and attain communion with the Father." Over the centuries the Church has applied this treasury in the form of pardon for past offenses and inducement to do some good work, allowing the person benefiting to apply benefits gained to himself or souls in purgatory. Indulgences are also rooted in one other Catholic doctrine — the Power of the Keys. This is the power given by Jesus to Peter as head of His Church, which Catholics believe is passed on from Peter through his successors, the popes. Mt 16:17-19 clearly states this power which binds and looses not only on earth but also in heaven. Fundamentalists may deny this power, but the Catholic Church accepts it at face value, and believing as it does, it is not surprising that it uses it.

94

Nor is the idea illogical. The notion that a misdeed can be made up by good behavior exists in most families, and even civil law is assigning community service for prison sentences in many cases. Popes using the power of the keys began decreeing that certain works useful for the common good could replace penitential practices. The Council of Nicea in 325 ruled that under certain conditions bishops could grant leniency to sinners in return for some good work. When the First Crusade was proclaimed, the Council of Clermont ruled that if Crusaders, from a worthy motive, "set out to liberate the Church of God in Jerusalem, that journey shall be counted as satisfaction for every penance" (plenary indulgence). True, there have been abuses of indulgences, as in the case of Tetzel, but each time the Church moved to correct them.

The latest revision of indulgences was made by Pope Paul VI as the result of the Vatican Council. His constitution released in 1967 lays down current norms. An indulgence may be partial or full (plenary). A partial indulgence is no longer measured in a time period, and the amount of penalty remitted is left to God. Indulgences may be gained for oneself or applied to the dead by way of suffrage. No indulgence can be applied to another living person. To gain an indulgence one must be baptized, not excommunicated, and in the state of grace (free of sin). To obtain a plenary indulgence requires that all attachment to sin, even venial sin, be absent. In addition the following three conditions must be met: confession, eucharistic communion, prayer for the pope's intention.

The actions and prayers to which indulgences are attached are printed in the *Manual (Enchiridion) of Indulgences*, which can be bought in any Catholic book store. Anyone reading these prayers and deeds will readily see that rather than undermining spirituality, as opponents of indulgences claim, they are all designed to increase spirituality and bring one closer to God.

12

Mary

Worship of Mary is Babylonian in origin. We blaspheme when we intrude Mary into a mediatory role that belongs solely to Jesus. Mary is not the mother of God.

Scripture teaches us that we should worship no one else but God. Jesus reemphasized this teaching when tempted by Satan. Promised all the kingdoms of the world if He will bow down before Satan in worship, Jesus, quoting Deuteronomy 6:13, tells the tempter that worship belongs only to "the Lord your God and him only shall you serve." To give worship to anyone else but God becomes a form of idolatry. Hence, many non-Catholic Christians become disturbed, and in many cases irate, at the honor and respect Catholics give to Mary and the saints, interpreting this as the worship due only to God.

Actually, the word "worship" is a bit awkward in itself. Webster's Collegiate Dictionary cites four meanings to the word: 1. honor or reverence given to a divine being; 2. a religious practice, creed or ritual; 3. admiration for an object of esteem; 4. British usage as a title for a person of importance (judge, mayor, bishop). The distinctions made by Catholic theologians seem clearer. They divide worship this way: *latria*, the adoration due only to God — Father, Son and Holy Spirit — as creator and ruler; *dulia*, the respect and honor given to angels and saints; *hyperdulia*, a higher respect and honor given to Mary because she was specially chosen by the Father to be the mother of His Son; *civilitas*, the special courtesy and respect given to outstanding men and women as civil honor.

The Church honors Mary because she was a unique woman, who was blessed among all women; who by her life found favor with God (Lk 1:28); whose "Let it be done to me" ceded her free will to God and enabled her to become the mother of His Son, thus having a share in our redemption (Lk 1:38); and who because of her consent would be called blessed by all ages to come (Lk 1:48).

Mary is the fulfillment of the Old Testament, the last of a line of favored women in the Bible: at the beginning, Eve, the mother of humanity; Sarah, mother of the line from which Jesus would spring, blessed in her advanced age as would be the mothers of Samson, Samuel, and John the Baptist; Deborah, Judith, Esther, whom God chose to save His people. When the time came for God's final fulfillment of our redemption, Mary was the one chosen to become the mother of the Redeemer. She is the woman who nurtures Him at birth, carries Him to the safety in Egypt, guards Him in childhood, cares for Him in His hidden years, is the cause of His first miracle at Cana, follows Him on His mission, stands beneath His cross, and fulfills the prophecy of Simeon; and finally awaits the coming of the Holy Spirit with His disciples.

Who then can resent the honor given to this chosen woman of God? It is a reverence and love Catholics share with many Protestants. Anglicans kept intact the Church's devotion to Blessed Mary. The German Evangelical *Adult Catechism* in treating of Mary under the heading "Mary Belongs in the Gospel" says:

"Mary is not only 'Catholic'; but she is also 'Evangelical.' Protestants tend to forget that. But Mary clearly is the mother of Jesus and closer to him than the closest disciples. With what humanity the New Testament depicts this closeness, without concealing Mary's distance from Jesus! An example of this distance can be seen in Luke, who tells so much about Mary. A woman from the crowd says to Jesus: 'Blest is the womb that bore you and the breasts that nursed you!' Jesus replies: 'Blest are they who hear the word of God and keep it' (11:27-28). But does not that apply precisely to Mary? She is depicted as exemplary hearer of God's word, as the handmaid of the Lord who says 'Yes' to the will of God, as the blessed one who is nothing of herself but gains everything through God's goodness. Mary is the pattern for men who let themselves be opened and gifted by God, of the community of believers, of the Church."

To give Mary this honor and respect takes nothing from the sole salvific role the Father willed for Jesus, a salvation Mary shares in with all other humans. Yet Mary's "Yes" gives her a role in that salvation possessed by no other human, Apostle or saint. Moreover, through her life she becomes a model of what the Church should be. "Devoutly meditating on her," says Vatican Council II, "and contemplating her in the light of the Word made man, the Church reverently penetrates more deeply into the great mystery of the Incarnation and becomes more and more like her spouse. Having entered deeply into the history of salvation, Mary, in a way, unites in her person and re-echoes the most important doctrines of the faith: and when she is the subject of preaching and worship she prompts the faithful to come to her Son, to his sacrifice, and the love of the Father" (*Lumen Gentium*, 65).

Mother of God

Mary is not the mother of God. She is only the mother of the human Jesus. It was not God who was born in Bethlehem but "the man Christ Jesus" (1 Tim 2:5).

All the fundamentalists I know would agree with the above statement, although I would hope they would disagree with the misapplication of Paul's teachings and beliefs. They are willing to admit that Jesus is God, but they shudder at that beautiful title given Mary by the Eastern Churches, *Theotokos* (God-bearer). The position of these fundamentalists is not original with them; it was one of the early heresies in the Church, Nestorianism. Bishop Nestorius was condemned and deposed by the Council of Ephesus, which ruled: "If anyone does not confess that the Word of God the Father was united to a body by hypostasis and that one is Christ with his own body, the same one evidently both God and man, let him be anathema." The heresy arose again at various times and has been resurrected in our own day.

The Church does not say that Mary is the mother of the Father or of the Holy Spirit but solely the mother of the second person of the Trinity, Jesus Christ. Before His Incarnation Jesus was pure spirit as is the Father and Holy Spirit. In a humbling act that no human mind can comprehend, the second person of the Trinity was joined to a human body, subject to all the laws of nature, and became God-man. It was as God-man that Jesus arose from the dead after His crucifixion, and it is as God-man that He rules today in heaven, promising to return to earth again at the end of time.

If Jesus Christ is God and Mary is not the mother of God, then Jesus has to be two persons — a human person and a divine person. But no fundamentalist holds that Jesus is two people. The distinction theologians make is that Jesus is one person with two natures — a human nature and a divine nature, joined together in the hypostatic union. Mary is the mother of the human nature, but because Jesus is one person and Mary is the mother of that person, Mary is the mother of God. Because the Incarnation is mystery, not fully understandable to the human mind, we do not know exactly what happens in the Incarnation, but we do know what has resulted, that human nature is essentially united with divinity. Perhaps the fundamentalist error arises because the hypostatic union is mystery and what is not understandable is to be rejected; yet if this were to be followed to its ultimate conclusion, it would deny God Himself.

Mary Our Mediatrix

Mary as mediatrix is another Catholic teaching that fundamentalists cannot accept. They affirm that there is only one mediator with the Father and that is Jesus Christ. This is true, but that does not prevent Mary from assisting Jesus in His mediation. When a fundamentalist prays for another, he is in effect being a mediator himself, and his mediation takes nothing from the Lord. It is Mary's great desire to bring all people to her Son, and thus she prays for them and acts on their behalf.

Vatican Council II teaches: "The motherhood of Mary in the order of grace continues uninterruptedly from the consent which she loyally gave at the Annunciation and which she sustained without wavering beneath the cross, until the eternal fulfillment of all the elect. Taken up to heaven, she did not lay aside this saving office but by her manifold intercession continues to bring us the gifts of eternal salvation. By her maternal charity she continues to care for the brethren of her Son, who still journey on earth surrounded by dangers and difficulties, until they are led into their blessed home. Therefore the Blessed Virgin is invoked in the Church under the titles of Advocate, Helper, Benefactress, and Mediatrix. This, however, is so understood that it neither takes away anything or adds anything to the dignity and efficacy of Christ the one Mediator" (*Lumen Gentium*, 64).

Mediation is carried on at all levels of the communion of saints, but she who took part in His redeeming labors and shared in His sorrow makes her the highest example outside Jesus in the communion of saints. She is a model for all Christians, praying that they will unite their lives with the life of her Son. In Mary's actions His power is revealed, for she has nothing apart from her divine Son. Jesus, who lives to make intercession for us (Heb 7:27), sharing His mediating efforts with His mother, just as He shared His life on earth with her. Mary's mediation with her Son began at Cana and continues to this day.

Mary, Ever-Virgin

While Mary was a virgin when Jesus was born, she did not remain a virgin, for the Bible tells us she had other children.

The Catholic Church teaches as an article of faith that Mary remained perpetually a virgin. The Church has defined this in various councils, and since Catholics believe the promise of Jesus to keep the Church from error through the infusion of the Holy Spirit, that is enough for them. However, this is not enough for fundamentalists and other Protestants who do not accept the authority of the Church. How then is the Bible to be explained?

The New Testament in a number of places refers to brothers and sisters of Jesus (Mt 12:46ff, Mk 3:31, Lk 8:19, Jn 7:3, Acts 1:14, 1 Cor 9:5); four are expressly named — Joses, Simon, Jude, and James (who became first bishop of Jerusalem). However, careful reading will reveal that *nowhere does Scripture say that these are children of Mary*. Indeed, Scripture seems to indicate otherwise. In the account of finding Jesus in the Temple, the narration reads as that of an only child. Mk 6:3 refers to Jesus as "son of Mary," a scriptural usage of the only son of a widow, otherwise Joseph would have been mentioned. Finally, on the cross Jesus entrusted Mary to the care of John, an unnatural act if there were other children.

Some critics reply to these arguments, "But Luke 2:7 refers to Jesus as firstborn son, indicating that other children followed." Such a conclusion is an abuse of interpretation. "Firstborn" was a Jewish technical term for the child who opened the womb and was specially consecrated to God (see Ex 13:2, Lk 2:23). The term has a precise meaning and does not mean the first of a series. Archaeologists working in the Holy Land uncovered a tomb inscription from the period which commemorates a woman who died giving birth to her "firstborn."

Finally, there is the argument from the tradition of the early Church. The Apostles' Creed refers to the virginity of Mary; the Confiteor calls her "ever virgin," as does the exposition of Epiphanus on the Nicene Creed. Pope St. Siricus (384) condemns those who say Mary had other children and calls it a denial of faith. The belief in Mary's perpetual virginity could certainly not have developed in the early Church if one son was the Bishop of Jerusalem and other children prominent Christians. Yet this belief is attested to by apostolic writers — Irenaeus, Polycarp, Ignatius, among others.

If these brothers and sister of Jesus were not children of Mary, who were their parents? Some have suggested that they were children of Joseph by an earlier marriage and that they were half-brothers and half-sisters of Jesus. There is no indication of this in Scripture. Although the perpetual virginity of Joseph has never been defined by the Church, it is Church tradition that he was always a virgin.

The Church's explanation has always been that James and the others were cousins of Jesus. Neither Hebrew nor Aramaic had a word for cousin, hence the term brother or sister was used for any degree of relationship (Lv 10:4, 1 Chr 23:22, Gn 13:8, etc.). Although the New Testament was written in Greek, it would have been natural for Hebrew and Aramaic mentalities to use the terms brother and sister when they mean kinsmen.

It is not clear who were the parents of these cousins. The crucifixion accounts may give some indication. Matthew mentions the women who had followed the ministry of Jesus being there, among them "Mary Magdalene and Mary, the mother of James and Joses (Joseph), and the mother of the sons of Zebedee (James and John). Mark's list gives Mary Magdalene, Mary, the mother of the younger James and Joses, and Salome. Luke gives no list. John does not mention women from Galilee but says that near the cross of Jesus "were his mother and his mother's sister, Mary the wife of Clopas, and Mary Magdala." Matthew and Mark in naming children evidently presumed their readers would know who these children were.

Despite the three accounts, it is not clear whether there were three or four women there. If there were only three women, "his mother's sister" becomes Mary the wife of Clopas, the mother of James and Joses. If there were four women, "his mother's sister" could be Salome, and her sons, previously identified as James and John, would be Jesus' first cousins, or the fourth woman could be Mary, the mother of James and Joses, but not the wife of Clopas. While there is no way for us to solve the problem, St. Jerome, author of the Vulgate, held that there were only three women and states that Clopas is the same as Alphaeus and the father of the second James in the list of Apostles. Hegesippus, a second century writer, states that Clopas was St. Joseph's brother, the uncle of Jesus and the father of Simon and Jude. Thus the "brothers and sisters of the Lord" could involve several sets of cousins with different parentages. As Anna's King of Siam was fond of saying, "It's a puzzlement."

13

Saints and Images

Catholic practice of worshiping saints is a continuation of ancient heathen beliefs. Romanism is patently guilty of worshiping false gods — a practice condemned repeatedly in Scripture.

In scholastic debate it is considered bad form to categorically deny an opponent's major premise. Yet when a major premise is proven false, the whole argument collapses. That is the case with the above statement, with one false assertion after another. Catholics are forbidden by the first commandment of God to adore saints, images, or anything else but God Himself. What Catholics give to saints and images is veneration, the same veneration you would give to your mother, the American flag, or a statue of George Washington.

It is true that throughout the Old Testament there is condemnation after condemnation against images. However, this condemnation must be understood in context. The Jewish people were surrounded by pagan people, each tribe with its own gods, which the people had represented in images. These idols are what Scripture is talking about because by bringing such images into Israel people would be forsaking the Lord for strange and false gods. An example of the Lord's displeasure with such a practice is given in 1 Kings 11. Solomon had married foreign wives for political alliances, and these wives introduced their false gods into Israel. The Lord was angry with Solomon and told him that because he did not keep the laws given him, Solomon's kingdom would be given to another. This was a man who in his younger years built the first temple for the Lord, and the Lord approved of it and renewed the covenant made with David (1 Kings 6:12). Yet in this same temple, Solomon placed images of angels, each made of olivewood ten cubits high. The biblical distinction between images and idols is clear. Solomon also had images of animals sculpted into his palace, and these were not condemned by God.

Catholics began using visual aids long, long before the term was coined. The greatest artists expressed their own faith in statues of Jesus, Mary, and the saints, not as objects to be adored or prayed to, but as reminders of those whom the art represented whose lives had proven pleasing to the Father. The art was a prompting to all to imitate saintly virtues and devotion to God. Who, standing before Michelangelo's great masterpiece the Pietà, is not moved by the suffering of Jesus and His mother? Painters left behind artistic interpretation of biblical scenes, lives of saints, and general religious topics, not only to express their own faith but to strengthen the faith and belief of the beholder. True, Catholics pray before these images, but they are not praying to the image but to what the image represents.

Catholics pay particular honor and respect to the cross and the crucifix for what they represent and find it difficult to understand Christian people avoiding them. Not too many years ago a Catholic church could always be recognized by the cross atop its steeple, a practice avoided in Protestant churches. Now some of the newer Protestant churches are adding a cross while still avoiding the crucifix in interior decoration, except for some Anglican practice and a few others. For Catholics, the cross only has its true meaning when it holds its Victim. Yes, Christ is now resurrected, triumphant, and reigning in heaven, but that is no reason that we should forget the sacrifice which won our redemption and salvation. So the crucifix is a mandated part of every Catholic church's interior decoration, a constant reminder that we have been bought at a great price.

The early Church used statues and images as aids to devotion and as expressions of faith. One need only to visit the catacombs in Rome to see statues and frescoes representing not only Christ but also scenes from Scripture. When the Church emerged from the catacombs, it continued to decorate its houses of worship with statues, mosaics, frescoes, and oil paintings, all designed to increase a spirit of prayerfulness. In the eighth century the Emperor Leo III of Constantinople led a movement against images, known as iconoclasm. Motivated partly by the spread of Islam, which denounced images, partly by politics, partly because of some superstition, and partly by a way to acquire gold and silver, Leo stripped images from churches and even private homes. The popes rejected this attack, and when the Empress Irene came to the throne iconoclasm was ended until resurrected by Protestant reformers. It became particularly virulent in Germany, Holland, and Britain, where walls were whitewashed, priceless paintings and statues destroyed, and stained-glass windows smashed. A carryover from the Reformation persists to this day.

That abuses arise is not to be denied. Superstition sometimes has crept in among simple, unlettered people who are not well versed in their faith and who fail to make the distinction between supposition and reality, often using religious objects as charms and amulets. Such practices are condemned by the Church as superstition and violation of the First Commandment of God. Such practices arise not from bad will but from lack of knowledge. We also find a mixture of Christian and pagan beliefs in such odd rites as voodoo, macumba, and santeria, practices which often have a great hold on a people nominally Catholic but ignorant of Catholic beliefs. Yet some who oppose the Catholic Church cite these aberrations as if they were a part of Catholicism, established by and approved by the Church, when in each case they are condemned.

It seems not to occur to the modern iconoclast that a person can bow down before a crucifix and not pray to the crucifix, that a person could kneel before a statue of Mary and not pray to the statue but the one whom the statue represents. They seem to have no difficulty with visitors to Washington standing before the statue of Lincoln in his great memorial and understanding that the visitors are not venerating the statue but the one whom the statue represents. Unless they are Jehovah's Witnesses, they will approve saluting the flag as patriotic, understanding that this is not worship of the flag but respect for what the flag represents. Yet Catholic respect is turned into idolatry.

If St. Paul could ask his Christians to pray for him (Rom 15:30 and elsewhere) or I could ask a fundamentalist to pray for me, why can I not ask the mother of Jesus to pray for me? I once read a fundamentalist response to this question in which the author ridiculed the idea, saying that prayers coming to the Blessed Virgin from all over the world would simply be a babble of voices, not understandable, as if heaven had a big switchboard that could become overloaded. Heaven is not to be thought of in terms limited to this world. There is neither space nor time in heaven, and God's power in regard to His saints is unlimited. If fundamentalists would make an effort to understand Catholic teaching on the Communion of Saints and the Mystical Body of Christ (Jn 15), they might better appreciate Catholic reasoning. If Jesus is the vine and the faithful the branches, one does not cease being a member of this vine because of worldly death. Life as part of the vine continues even in heaven.

Non-Catholics find difficulty with the Catholic Church's reverence for and veneration of saints, which they frequently label as superstition. In the Apostolic Church all Christians were called saints, the holy people of God, thus Paul begins his letter to the Colossians: "To the saints and faithful brethren in Christ at Colossae." In the early post-Apostolic Church the term became limited to martyrs and men and women of eminent holiness. Today the Church recognizes all those in heaven as saints, but honor is limited to those officially canonized (Greek, *kanon*, list or rule), that is, listed in the Church's calendar of saints. In the early days of the Church there were no formal procedures, but saints became recognized through miracles and popular acclaim. Today, popular acclaim leads to more formal procedures.

Canonization is a declaration by the pope, which Catholics regard as infallible, that a person who died as a martyr and/or exhibited virtue to a heroic degree is now in heaven and worthy of honor and imitation. Such a declaration only comes after a long-drawn-out process, which begins first in the diocese where the person resided. After the cause, as it is called, is approved by the bishop, a postulator of the cause starts gathering evidence of the heroic life of the deceased by interviewing witnesses and examining any writing or talks. When this evidence is assembled it is forwarded to the Congregation for Saints in Rome, where it is examined and tested. If approved, the person is declared Venerable. The second step, called beatification, reexamines the person's life in greater detail, with the postulator arguing the person's sanctity while an official of the congregation (popularly called the devil's advocate) tries to dispute. At this stage there must be certification of an attested and proven miracle worked by God through the person's intercession. If this stage is approved, the pope decrees the servant of God to be Blessed, and local or limited liturgical honor can be given. The process then enters a third and final stage, which involves another detailed investigation of the person's holiness and another miracle through intercession to the Blessed. If this stage is completed favorably, the pope by infallible declaration declares the person has practiced heroic virtue to such a degree and led so blameless a life that he or she is now in heaven and is worthy of honor and imitation.

Because of the holiness of the saint, anything connected with the holy one is held in honor and is known as a relic (something left behind). This is not unusual even apart from the Church. The grave of George Washington is a place of patriotic pilgrimage. One can go to the Smithsonian Museum in Washington and see gowns worn by first ladies or Benjamin Franklin's spectacles. Relics are classified by the Church as first-, second-, and third-class. A first-class relic is the corpse of the saint or any part of it. A second-class relic is anything intimately connected with the saint, such as his Bible, a prayer book, etc. A third-class relic is anything that is touched to the body of a saint. Because of abuses in the past, the Church is very strict in its regulation and verification of relics, placing their veneration under the monitoring and regulation of the Congregation for Divine Worship. In the Code of Canon Law which governs the Church, Canon 1190 absolutely forbids the sale or alienation (illegal transfer) of sacred relics. The code also specifies penalties to be inflicted on those who profane a sacred thing or alienate an ecclesiastical good.

Finally, a word should be said about shrines and miracles, since these are often subjects of confusion. Among the better-known shrines of the western world are those at Lourdes, France; Fatima, Portugal; and Guadalupe in Mexico City. At each of these shrines the Blessed Virgin is said to have appeared: at Lourdes to St. Bernadette Soubirous, at Fátima to three young children, and at Tepeyac (Guadalupe) to the Indian Juan Diego.

Each of these shrines is known for the many miracles worked there on behalf of pilgrims. The Catholic Church teaches that public revelation ended with the Apostles. Private revelation continues, but none of it has ever been defined, and thus Catholics are not held to its belief. Thus the declarations of the Virgin said to have taken place at these shrines are open to belief or disbelief by Catholics. However, because of an unending stream of pilgrims to these and other shrines, the faith exhibited by these pilgrims, and the spiritual fruits gained there, the Church does hold these places in reverence.

Lourdes is a good example of a place where thousands of spiritual conversions have taken place and hundreds of physical miracles of the sick have given new life. From its earliest days there was set up at Lourdes a medical board to examine reputed physical cures, staffed by doctors and scientists, who investigated the history of a cured person's illness and, only after ruling out self-suggestion and hysteria, would declare a cure miraculous and beyond human explanation.

The validity of cures at Lourdes was attested to by Dr. Alexis Carrel, an American surgeon and biologist, who had been born in France but came to America and joined the Rockefeller Institute. For his pioneer work in suturing blood vessels, in transfusions, and transplants, he was awarded the Nobel Prize in Physiology and Medicine. He also pioneered work on an artificial heart. While on a vacation to his homeland he went to Lourdes out of curiosity and as a skeptic. Doctors at the Lourdes Bureau, aware of his reputation, invited him to examine their work. Among the cases he saw was a woman near death who arrived at Lourdes with an inoperable cancerous tumor. She went into the Lourdes water and when she emerged the cancer was gone. Carrel wrote about this and other Lourdes experiences when he returned to America, declaring himself a firm believer in Lourdes.

In Catholic teaching, miracles are "observable events or effects in the physical or moral order of things which cannot be explained by the ordinary operation of the laws of nature and which, therefore, are attributed to the direct action of God" (*Catholic Almanac*). God worked miracles through human agency in the Old Testament. The Gospels are full of the miracles of Jesus Christ. The Book of Acts show miracles worked through the Apostles. The Church believes that God works miracles as aids to salvation. God, who is the Author of the laws of nature, can set aside these laws to manifest His divine power, again sometimes working through human means. Simply because a thing is not easily explained does not make it a miracle. The Church only accepts something as miraculous when every natural explanation has been tried and found wanting. A miracle of grace is a sudden and instantaneous conversion, such as happened to Paul on the road to Damascus.

To many non-Catholics much of the above may sound like a defense of superstition. Yet there is evidence for all that has been written. An unbiased study might well lead to surprising conclusions.

14

'Call No Man Father'

The Catholic church states that priests are called Gods (spelled with a capital "G"). The priest is a God who makes Gods. Celibacy is both unscriptural and the cause of much tragic immorality. The Bible tells us to call no one on earth our father.

The first two sentences above are taken directly from a book by Jimmy Swaggart attacking Catholicism. I challenge Mr. Swaggart or anyone else to produce any statement of the Catholic Church, made in its nearly two thousand years of history, that ever referred to a priest as God, capital or small letter. The accusation is laughable to Catholics and only reveals the unschooled bias of a self-appointed prophet. There is only one God, uncreated, existing for all eternity, and the creator of all things that existed, are existing, or will exist outside Himself.

It is difficult to understand the fundamentalist's disturbed concern over priests. The accusation that the priest stands as a barrier between God and the Christian in the pew, to be logical, would have to be made against any minister, rabbi, imam, or spiritual leader, including one's own minister or leader. The charge that the priesthood developed from paganism forgets the priesthood of the Old Covenant and its establishment in the New as the third order of leadership, as was discussed earlier.

Fundamentalists love to quote Mt 23:9 to Catholics they are hoping to influence: "Call no man your father on earth, for you have one Father, who is in heaven." Is the Bible then disobeying Jesus in Mark 9:14-29 (and elsewhere) when it uses the word father in a number of places to describe the man who brought his son to Jesus, hoping for a miracle?

In reading the Bible we have to understand what is behind the words, otherwise what we read is subject to misinterpretation. The verse cited above must be taken in its context to be understood. The verse is part of a passage in which Jesus is excoriating the Jewish establishment which opposed Him. He accuses the members of this group of idle formalism and vain display, always seeking high places, always wanting honors and titles. He condemns their use of three titles: *rabbi* (master), *abba* (father), and *moreh* (teacher). He was indicating that these men who were seeking His death did not deserve the titles given them: they were masters of nothing; they were not true fathers because they didn't care for their people, grinding them down under impossible burdens; they taught falsehood. In short, they were not worthy of the titles they demanded. He also meant that there is one true Father, God; and one Master and Teacher, Himself. Jesus did not mean that you shouldn't call your dad your father or not refer to your teacher in school as your teacher. To affirm this is to destroy the whole point Jesus is making.

Christian Tradition from the first days has interpreted this verse in its restricted sense, that Christians should not seek worldly honors but should be servants of one another. St. Paul was probably the first to use the word "father" in the sense that Catholics apply to their priests. In 1 Cor C:15 he writes to his Corinthians: "For I became your father in Christ Jesus through the gospel." St. Paul considered himself the father of the Church in Corinth because through his preaching and baptisms the Corinthians were brought to new life in Christ. It is in this sense that Catholics use the title in reference to their priests, because through the priest's hands people are brought to new life through Baptism. Just as a natural father serves the material needs of his family, the priest serves the spiritual needs of the parish to which he is assigned. The use of the term in this

Pauline sense takes nothing away from God the Father and in this restricted sense does not contradict Matthew.

Celibacy is another sore point with fundamentalists, although why an imitation of Jesus and St. Paul should be condemned is not understandable. Celibacy is a discipline only in the Western church; priests (not bishops) in the Eastern Church are allowed to be married. It was not always a universal Western discipline, and early popes and priests were married. The Council of Elvira (Spain) in 306 ruled that bishops, priests, and deacons should be celibate and those already married should "keep away from their wives and not beget children." Pope Hadrian I, in a letter to Spain condemning various abuses, berated false priests who "choose women for themselves in marriage." The first Lateran Council (1123) ruled that all priests, deacons, and subdeacons could only live in a house with a woman if that woman was "a mother, sister, paternal or maternal aunt, or others of this kind concerning whom no suspicion should arise." The Church had not only adopted celibacy but also the means to protect it.

It was Jesus who gave the first call to celibacy. In discussing marriage with His disciples, He told them (Mt 19:11-12) that "Not all men can receive this precept, but only those to whom it is given. For there are eunuchs who have been so from birth, and there are eunuchs who have been made eunuchs by men, and there are eunuchs who have made themselves eunuchs for the sake of the kingdom of heaven. He who is able to receive this, let him receive it." Jesus was not placing a mandate on His followers but a counsel. Celibacy was for those able to keep it for the perfection of the kingdom of heaven, where the saved "neither marry nor are given in marriage, but are like angels in heaven" (Mt 22:30).

St. Paul took this counsel as a model for his own life. In his discussion of marriage (1 Cor 7) he observes, "It is well for a man not to touch a woman." Being a realist, however, Paul recognized that celibacy was not for all. He concludes (7-9): "I wish all were as I myself am. But each has his own special gift from God, one of one kind and one of another. . . . To the unmarried and the widows I say that it is well for them to remain single as I do. But if they cannot exercise self-control they should marry. For it is better to marry than be aflame with passion."

Thus the Western Church in mandating the discipline of celibacy for its priests (a deacon is permitted to be married when ordained, but if his wife dies, the deacon cannot remarry) is carrying out the counsel of Jesus and the wish of St. Paul. It is Catholic belief that God gives each person a vocation in life (1 Cor 7:17) and sufficient grace to live that vocation as long as one cooperates with its grace. Thus while celibacy is difficult, God's grace is sufficient to enable the priest to live this life and devote himself totally to his work. Paul recognized this when he wrote: "The unmarried man is anxious about the affairs of the Lord, how to please the Lord; but the married man is anxious about worldly affairs, how to please his wife, and his interests are divided" (1 Cor 7:32-33). Celibacy is not only biblical in origin but also a gift of the Spirit, just as faithful married love is a gift of the Spirit.

The charge is not infrequently placed that celibacy is against nature. It is made because one of the fallacies of modern thinking is that people cannot control their sexual drives. Jesus in recommending celibacy does not ask the impossible and the grace of God is sufficient (2 Cor 12:9). Moreover, a priest who commits himself to celibacy does so only after intellectual and spiritual training that lasts a number of years, at the end of which through reflection and prayer he has reached the firm conclusion through practice that Christ is giving him this gift for the good of the Church and his service to others.

Much is made by some non-Catholics of the failure of a few priests to maintain their vow of celibacy. Does one condemn the apostolic band for the failure of one member? Why then should the priesthood be condemned because of the failure of a few? When a failure happens, the man is asked to leave the priesthood. He can apply to Rome to be reduced to the lay state and be allowed to marry. When such a failure does occur, it arises from a diminution in one's spiritual life and its consequent loss of grace. The priest who fails is more to be pitied than condemned. A few (very few) who leave provide fodder for anti-Catholics in an attempt to justify their own defection. They are celebrated by enemies of the Church because they are oddities, but their sponsors can be assured that in leaving the ex-priest followed an invariable pattern — a loss of prayer life, an involvement in the world, and finally an abandonment of his sacred vow to the Lord to be celibate.

Those who believe in the totality of the word of God — the Bible — should be supportive of it when it speaks of celibacy and not critical of those who accept its counsels. To do less calls their whole religious rationale into question.

15

The Inquisition

In totality, it is estimated that the Roman Catholic church murdered some twenty million people during the existence of the Inquisition.

The word inquisition comes from the Latin, meaning to inquire. It is difficult to write about the Inquisition in a few pages because of the complexity of the subject and the misinformation that has been spread abroad, like the ludicrous statement above, which is taken from a current anti-Catholic text. But even that is conservative to Ralph Woodrow's ninety-five million killed, a figure that equaled the total population of Europe in 1650, given perhaps on the theory that if you are going to tell a lie, it might as well be a big one. The standard Protestant author on the Inquisition is Henry C. Lea, whose scholarship is marred for impartial historians because of his anti-Catholic bias and his basic failure to distinguish between various inquisitions.

Before discussing the Inquisition, two points need to be made. The first is that the American view of history is largely a white Anglo-Saxon Protestant one. The role of the Spanish and later blacks in our history has largely been ignored. I attended public schools, and I first believed that the United States was settled by English pilgrims in 1620. Later a teacher said that this wasn't so; English settlers had come to Jamestown in Virginia in 1607. Only when I was out of public schools did I realize that it wasn't the English but the Spanish who had come first. I discovered that the first Catholic martyr of what was to be the United States died in 1542 in central Kansas, that the Spanish had tried to establish a colony near what was to be Jamestown in 1570 but had it decimated by Indians; and that in 1565 St. Augustine, Florida, was founded and is the oldest city in the United States. All of this was unknown to children with whom I went to school.

We had received a WASP view of English history that traces itself back to the Reformation and to the political and religious rivalry between Protestant England and Catholic Spain. This gave rise to the English "Black Legend," which painted anything Spanish in the darkest of terms and in colors of craftiness, cruelty, and coarseness, all in the contempt of caricature. English history on the other hand was a cavalcade of cheerfulness worthy of a Pollyanna. The English feted their Good Queen Bess, although on the continent she was known as Bloody Bess. English history told of the horrors of Spanish dungeons but was silent about the tortures in the Tower of London and other English prisons that saw so many Catholics sent forth from them to be hanged, drawn, and quartered. England's Toleration Act freed non-Anglican Protestant nonconformists from the rigors of the Penal Laws in 1689, but Catholic emancipation did not come until 1829.

The second thing that must be remembered is that history has to be evaluated according to the mentality of the times in which it took place. The years of the Reformation and Counter-Reformation were harsh years when human rights as we know them today were not considered. Civil punishment was often cruel and sadistic. The rack, the iron maiden, and other devices of torture were standard ways to obtain confessions. The death penalty was often rendered for even simple thefts. Very, very few people ever questioned these cruelties, which today we consider horrors. Today, from a distance, we can declare those times to be a terrible period, but for people who lived through them they were ordinary times. All of the above must be kept in mind when speaking of the Inquisition.

When someone brings up the Inquisition as a way of attacking Catholicism, my response is always a question: "Which Inquisition are you talking about?" This always brings a puzzled look on the accuser's face and reveals that the subject has not been really studied. It is usually news when such people are told that there were a number of inquisitions, those of the Middle Ages and later the Spanish Inquisition and Roman Inquisition, the latter still existing in the present Roman Congregation for the Doctrine of the Faith.

If you really want to set such people aback, a sure way to do it is to tell them that the various inquisitions started out as a biblical response, and it is true. In one of His training sessions of the Twelve, Jesus told them, "Do not fear those who kill the body but cannot kill the soul; rather fear him who can destroy both soul and body in hell" (Mt 10:28). Hence, people who propagated heresy and led others astray were considered very dangerous people because they were leading others to hell unless repentance was made. Hence, authorities rationalized these subverters of faith were to be sought out, persuaded to see their errors, brought to repentance, and restored to life in the Church. Thus the inquisitions started out from good motives but in some cases became perverted for personal or political motives, and when such perversions take place they should be condemned by Catholics and Protestants alike.

The Middle Ages Inquisitions

The first inquisitions were entrusted to bishops in Southern France against the Albigensians, who propagated a doctrine of Manichaeanism and Gnosticism that among other things denied the divinity of the human Jesus. The bishops were ineffective, and in 1198 a second inquisition was turned over to Cistercian monks. Finally in 1233 Pope Gregory IX established a new inquisition and entrusted it to Dominican friars. An inquisitor would come into a region and announce that all guilty of heresy had a month to recant. Those that did were given a light penance and dismissed. Those accused who did not recant were brought to trial. Torture was sometimes used to extract a confession, although Pope Nicholas I had issued an edict against its introduction.

The *New Columbia Encyclopedia* in describing this Inquisition says: "The verdict and sentence of the inquisitor were enforced by the local ruler only; heresy was considered a civil as well as spiritual offense. Burning at the stake was thought to be the fitting punishment for unrecanted heresy, probably through the analogy of the Roman law on treason. However, burning of heretics was not common in the Middle Ages; the usual punishments were penance, fine, and imprisonment. A verdict of guilty also meant the confiscation of property by the civil ruler, who might turn part of it over to the church. "

That the practice led to some abuse is not to be denied, but "The inquisitors," says the encyclopedia, "were eager to receive abjurations of heresy and avoid trials; their purpose was to win back heretics." Civil rulers on the other hand used the trials as opportunities to enrich themselves and settle grudges, as did some enemies of the accused. After a hundred years of preaching by the Dominicans and local clerical reform, the Albigensian heresy disappeared and this Inquisition came to an end.

The Roman Inquisition

In 1542 Pope Paul III established the Roman Inquisition to counteract what he saw as Protestant heresies being propagated from Germany and Switzerland. This inquisition was entrusted to the Congregation of the Holy Office, today known as the Congregation for the Doctrine of the Faith, charged then as now with conserving and promotion of Catholic orthodoxy. Because of past experience, this Inquisition was kept independent of civil and secular powers. It had as its aim showing people in doctrinal error their mistakes and leading them back to orthodoxy. It had detailed legal procedures that had to be followed, and although some abuses did creep in here and there, particularly away from Rome, they were immediately corrected when brought to the attention of the Holy See. Historically, the most celebrated case brought before the Roman Inquisition was that of Galileo.

The Galileo Case

Although the case of Galileo Galilei (1564-1642) is usually represented as a clash between science and religion, it was actually more subtle than that, arising from a mistaken fundamentalist interpretation of the Bible. The cosmology of the Old Testament was very primitive, imagining the earth as a flat plain set in an endless sea of water on columns of the earth. Beneath the earth was *sheol*, the place of the dead. Rising from the earth were floodgates, a great wall below which was the firmament of the sky with the sun, moon, and stars, and above it, beneath heaven, waters which rained down upon earth when God opened the floodgates. This cosmology was updated as the centuries passed but it was basically Ptolemaic — in which the earth was the center of the universe and the sun moved around the earth.

The Polish astronomer Copernicus disagreed with the prevalent teaching and through his studies concluded the earth and planets moved about the sun. He lectured in Rome on mathematics and astronomy. His monumental work, *The Revolutions of Celestial Orbs*, was written about 1530 and dedicated to Pope Paul III. It was not published, however, until 1543 when Copernicus was dying. Galileo accepted the theory and set about proving it with an astronomical telescope which he had constructed. In 1611 he displayed the telescope at the papal court and began propagating his findings. In 1616 the Inquisition found Copernicus's theory as dangerous to faith because it undermined biblical truth. Galileo was called to Rome and told not to promote Copernicanism.

In 1632 Galileo published a work meant not for scientists but for the general population that supported the Copernican system. He was summoned to Rome by the Inquisition and put on trial for undermining faith. Although he abjured what he had written, he was found guilty and sentenced to house arrest in Siena. Later he was permitted to move to Arcetri, near Florence. He was allowed to continue his studies, publishing his final book on physics in 1638, when blindness took over, and then death from age and illness followed. In our own time, Pope John Paul II removed the interdict placed against Galileo, admitting the Church's error. The Galileo incident is used by enemies of the Church to show that the Church is opposed to science, but the case was never about science, only about the denial of a supposed biblical truth that could destroy the ordinary man's belief in the Bible. I can imagine that those opposed to the Church can seize on this fact to prove that this mistaken notion of the sun moving around the earth only disproves that the Church is infallible. But a congregation of the Church does not possess infallibility, and even if the pope approved the congregation's finding, the pope is not infallible in matters of science, any more than you or I, but solely in matters of faith and morals, and then only under certain conditions.

The Spanish Inquisition

If the reader expects a defense of the Spanish Inquisition in these pages, it is not to be. Starting out from what might have been a legitimate motive, it turned into an instrument of terror. Ferdinand II, King of Aragon, married Isabella, Queen of Castile. The marriage brought all of Spain under their joint rule, except for those regions controlled by the Moors (African Moslems). They went to war to oust the Moors, and in 1492 (the same year their protégé Columbus discovered America) the last Moslem bastion, Granada, fell to their troops. They ordered all Jews and Moslems expelled from Spain, except for those who had converted to Christianity. Suspecting that many Moslems and some Jews only pretended conversion, they had earlier established the Spanish Inquisition to inquire into the legitimacy of these conversions, pressuring Pope Sixtus IV into naming an Inquisitor General. The *Columbia Encyclopedia* reports: "The popes were never reconciled to the institution, which they regarded as usurping a church prerogative."

The Spanish Inquisition soon became a political tool to rout out enemies of the state. An early inquisitor, the notorious Tomás de Torquemada, made his name synonymous with cruelty. No Spaniard was safe from its terror, even Church leaders. St. Ignatius Loyola and St. Teresa of Ávila were investigated for heresy. Unlike in the Middle Ages and Roman Inquisitions, the death penalty was freely applied and its tortures were notorious. The pope managed to keep the Spanish Inquisition out of Naples, of which Ferdinand was also king, but it was transplanted to the Spanish colonies in the New World and was particularly cruel in Mexico and some areas of South America, where it was used as an instrument to keep the population in subjection to Spanish rule and to put down any notions of rebellion. When the early nineteenth-century revolutions swept the countries of Latin America, Spanish rule came to an end, and so also did the Spanish Inquisition.

Although the Spanish Inquisition came into being in times that were more barbaric and cruel, that is no excuse for its excesses, just as there is no excuse for the Nazi extermination of so many in Europe. Although Spain was a Catholic country, as were its rulers, the Church did not control this Inquisition, which supposedly was to root out heresy but turned heresy into the politics of suppressed freedom and population control and was used to settle so many personal scores of those in charge. The

Spanish Inquisition is a black page in human history, and Catholics should deplore it, not because the Church was involved, which it wasn't, but because it was established and perpetuated by co-religionists to persecute other co-religionists.

16

No Salvation Outside the Church

Catholics are exclusive. They believe no one can be saved apart from their church. Catholic teaching is that all Protestants are destined to go to hell.

As I write, I have before me a letter from a Catholic mother who is very distraught. She has a son who is working in another city and who has left his Catholic faith to join a fundamentalist group there. This is disturbing enough for his mother, but what has really upset her is his assertion, "You are going to hell as long as you remain in the Catholic Church, the work of Satan."

"All my life I have tried to serve Jesus," this mother writes, "and I tried to bring my children up as good Christians. I don't know where I failed with this boy."

Writing back to this sad mother, I told her that if there was any failure, it was not her failure but that of her son. He is an adult, responsible for his own actions. Faith comes through grace, but to receive grace one must be open to it. Evidently her son had closed himself to grace and opened himself to new friends who led him into their religion and convinced him of their beliefs. What he said to his mother was very cruel but was consistent with fundamentalism's distaste for anything Catholic.

Having said all this, I would reject the charge that Catholics are exclusive but agree that it is Catholic teaching that there is no salvation outside the Catholic Church. The reasons for this are:

1. Jesus founded a Church.
2. That Church was to be the means of salvation for all

people of all nations throughout the earth for all time.

3. The Church Jesus founded is the Catholic Church.

4. Hence all people are called to be part of this Catholic unity.

The Fathers of Vatican Council II expanded on this "no salvation" statement when they said in their *Dogmatic Constitution on the Church*:

"Basing itself on scripture and tradition, it [the council] teaches that the Church, a pilgrim now on earth, is necessary for salvation: the one Christ is mediator and the way of salvation; he is present to us in his body which is the Church. He himself explicitly asserted the necessity of faith and baptism (cf. Mk 16:16, Jn 3:5), and thereby affirmed at the same time the necessity of the Church which men enter through baptism as through a door. Hence they could not be saved who, knowing the Catholic Church was founded as necessary by God through Christ, would refuse to enter it, or to remain in it."

Now before good-living Protestants cast me into the same cruel category as the mother's son, I would ask them to reread the last sentence directly above with care. For the no-salvation condemnation to apply, a person would have to know that the Catholic Church is the means God wills for salvation and, knowing this, reject the Church. This does not apply to most people outside the Catholic Church who are living their own beliefs in the certainty that this is what God wants of them.

The Council Fathers explain this in the paragraph that follows the one above, speaking first of Protestants, assuring them that the Church does not deny them the possibility of salvation, but through common beliefs sees them united in a special way to the Church.

"The Church knows she is joined in many ways to the baptized who are honored by the name Christian, but who do not profess the Catholic faith in its entirety or have not preserved unity or communion under the successor of Peter. For there are

126

many who hold sacred Scripture in honor as a rule of faith and life, who have a sincere religious zeal, who lovingly believe in God the Father Almighty and in Christ, the Son of God and the Savior, who are sealed by baptism which unites them to Christ."

But the Church reaches out even beyond Christians and declares salvation is also open to Jews, Moslems, and others:

"Finally, those who have not yet received the Gospel are related to the People of God in various ways. There is first the people to which the covenants and promises were made, and from which Christ was born according to the flesh (cf. Rom 9:4-5): in view of the divine choice, they are a people most dear for the sake of the fathers, for the gifts of God are without repentance (cf. Rom 11:28-29).

"But the plan of salvation also includes those who acknowledge their Creator, in the first place there are the Moslems: they profess to hold the faith of Abraham, and together with us adore the one, merciful God, mankind's judge on the last day. Nor is God remote from those who in shadows and images seek the unknown God, since he gives to all men life and breath and all things (cf. Acts 17:25-28), and since the Savior wills all men to be saved (cf. 1 Tim 2:4). Those who, through no fault of their own, do not know the Gospel of Christ or his Church, but nevertheless seek God with a sincere heart, and, moved by grace, try in their actions to do his will as they know it through the dictates of their conscience — those too may achieve salvation."

Thus, although God wills all to be saved through the Church founded by His Son, Jesus Christ, He still offers salvation out of a Father's love to those who strive to do His will as their consciences make it known to them. That offer of salvation would be lost, however, if the Church Christ founded was recognized but rejected out of bias or for some other personal reason, and it is for this reason that we say there is no salvation outside the Church.

So the Catholic position is far different from that of the fundamentalist son, who denies his mother salvation because she does not agree with his faith, circumscribed as it is with so many age-old prejudices and so much mindset, which is most tragic in the end because it places limitations on the grace of God.

That is why in the Preface this book began with a plea for an open mind, a dispassionate honesty that leaves room for the Spirit to enter.

Close yourself off and the Spirit is constrained, because God does not force Himself upon us.

Holman Hunt, the brilliant English painter and leader of the Pre-Raphaelite School, completed a religious painting that now hangs in Oxford University. It shows Christ knocking at a garden gate and was intended to illustrate Rev 3:20. Before showing the painting to the public, he invited some friends to a private viewing. One of these friends took him aside.

"Holman," the friend said, "you've made a serious error in your painting."

"An error?" asked Hunt.

"Yes. Your doorway has no knob or handle so one can enter."

"That is not a mistake," replied the artist. "The doorway represents the human heart. Christ is knocking on it but it must be opened from within if He is to enter."

So, too, is it with the Spirit's gifts. We must be amenable to accepting them.

In this book we have striven to show that the Catholic Church is rooted in the Bible and Apostolic Tradition. Nothing in the Church's teaching, its doctrine, its beliefs can contradict the Bible.

We have attempted to answer objections that fundamentalists in sincerity raise against that Church. We invite our fundamentalist brothers and sisters to examine the claims the Catholic Church makes, not with closed minds but with the openness of Christ, seeking only to do what the Master wills. We urge them to look, not at accidentals, but at the essence of the Church, which is Christ Himself, to find Him active in His sacraments and in His guidance, to experience the presence of the Holy Spirit who gives spiritual life to the faithful.

In the words of Jesus we bid you, "Come and see."

Recommended Bibliography

Holy Bible (Revised Standard Version, Catholic Edition), Thomas Nelson & Sons, 1965

The Catholic Almanac, ed. Felician A. Foy, O.F.M., Our Sunday Visitor, 1990

Vatican Council II: The Conciliar and Post Conciliar Documents, ed. Austin Flannery, O.P., Costello Publishing Co., 1975

Catholicism and Fundamentalism, Karl Keating, Ignatius Press, 1988

Fundamentals of Faith, Peter Kreeft, Ignatius Press, 1988

The Sources of Catholic Dogma, Henry Denziger, B. Herder Book Co., 1957

Evangelical Is Not Enough, Thomas Howard, Ignatius Press, 1984

The Words of Jesus in Our Gospels, Stanley B. Marrow, Paulist Press, 1979

The Church's Confession of Faith, German Bishops' Conference, Ignatius Press, 1987

The Maryknoll Catholic Dictionary, ed. Albert J. Nevins, M.M., Dimension Books, 1965

The Jerome Biblical Commentary, Prentice Hall, 1968

A New Catholic Commentary on Holy Scripture, Reginald C. Fuller, gen. ed., Nelson, 1969

The Teaching of Christ, ed. Ronald Lawler, O.F.M. Cap, Donald W. Wuerl, D.D., Thomas Comerford Lawler, Our Sunday Visitor, 1976

The Catholic Catechism, John C. Hardon, S.J., Doubleday, 1975

Strangers at Your Door, Albert J. Nevins, M.M., Our Sunday Visitor, 1988

The Beginnings of the Church, Frederick J. Cwiekowski, Paulist Press, 1988

Questions Catholics Ask, Frank Sheedy, Our Sunday Visitor, 1978

Ask Me a Question, Frank Sheedy, Our Sunday Visitor, 1989

The Catholic Church and the Bible, Peter M. J. Stravinskas, Our Sunday Visitor, 1987

The Church We Believe In, Francis A. Sullivan, S.J., Paulist Press, 1988

Catholic and Christian, Alan Schreck, Servant Books, 1984

The Code of Canon Law: A Text and Commentary, Paulist Press, 1985

The Didache (The Teaching of the Twelve Apostles), Paulist Press, 1948

Guide to the Vatican, Nino LoBello, Chicago Review Press, 1987

The Faith of Millions, John A. O'Brien, Our Sunday Visitor, 1963

Father Smith Instructs Jackson, John Francis Noll, Our Sunday Visitor, 1975

Index

Have you read
Cults, Sects, and the New Age?

This thoroughly researched book, by Rev. James J. LeBar, defines the term "cult," explains why cults are flourishing today, and discusses the history and beliefs of many major religious groups. Complete with Church documents and personal testimonies of former cult members. No. 431, paper, $7.95, 240 pp.

Other books from Father Nevins

Strangers At Your Door: How to Respond to Jehovah's Witnesses, the Mormons, Televangelists, Cults, and More, helps you protect yourself from the confusing teachings of evangelistic groups. It contains the history and beliefs behind many of the currently active sects and cults. Suggestions are provided for talking with members of these groups in a firm but charitable manner. No. 496, paper, $6.95, 144 pp.

American Martyrs features the biographies of all the American Catholic martyrs since 1542. This informative book examines the pioneer spirit and explains how the Catholic Faith was planted in the United States at the cost of many lives. No. 488, paper, $6.95, 180 pp.

A Saint For Your Name: Saints for Girls,
No. 321, paper, $5.95, 104 pp.

A Saint For Your Name: Saints for Boys,
No. 320, paper, $5.95, 120 pp.

Builders of Catholic America,
No. 582, paper, $7.95, 258 pp.

Called to Serve: A Guide Book for Altar Servers,
No. 663, paper, sold in packages of six, $13.95, 48 pp.

Life After Death,
No. 612, paper, $6.95, 156 pp.

Available from your local bookseller. For our complete catalog, or for more information please call 1-800-348-2440. From Indiana 219-356-8400. Our Sunday Visitor / 200 Noll Plaza / Huntington, IN 46750.